IF FALLING HEAD OVER HEELS
IN ... ...
DO ... ... ?

If you aren't deeply in love with someone, you are
missing the most exciting and enriching experience a man
or woman can know.

Yet so many factors—ranging from fear of rejection to a
host of self-defeating love games—can bar you
forever from this ultimate fulfillment.

Filled with fascinating case histories, revealing quizzes,
and wise, compassionate guidance, this book will
show you how to identify your problem, be it psychological
or sexual, and tell you how to free yourself of it.

Now you have a way that really works to light the flame
of romantic love for yourself and another person—
and keep it bright your whole life long.

IT CAN HAPPEN TO YOU

The Practical Guide to
ROMANTIC LOVE

More Reading from SIGNET and MENTOR

(0451)

IT CAN HAPPEN TO YOU

The Practical Guide to
Romantic Love

by
Dr. Roger Callahan
with
Karen Levine

Ⓞ
A SIGNET BOOK
NEW AMERICAN LIBRARY
TIMES MIRROR

To my kids—Patti, Amy, Martha, and Scott
—R.C.

To Alan, for all the right reasons
—K.L.

Acknowledgments

I would like to thank the individuals whose ideas and thinking have been of enormous benefit to me, personally and professionally: Bertrand Russell, the great romantic rationalist; Albert Ellis, the great rational-emotive clinician; and Nathaniel Branden, the clearest thinker and great explicator in the realm of romantic love.

Also, I wish to express appreciation to Frank Sinatra whose music, for two generations, has conveyed the agonies and ecstasies of romantic love as well as anyone ever has.

Contents

INTRODUCTION

WHEN I WAS EIGHTEEN, during World War II, I joined the Air Force and spent three years in the South Pacific. It was, of course, a tumultuous period, packed with experience. The men I lived with and fought beside helped to mold me as a person. Among the men I came to know, there were two in particular who made an indelible impression on me. These two men—John and Steven—were married and very much in love with their wives. Unlike most of the married men in my squadron, both were faithful to their wives; and the fact of their monogamy had nothing to do with religion, fear, or obligation. They didn't sleep with other women simply because they were in love with the women they had married.

Neither then nor now was I a great booster for the cause of monogamy for monogamy's sake. I have no particular moral or religious stand on that issue. But the kind of relationships that John and Steven had with their wives left me with a great respect for the concept of romantic love. My two Air Force buddies projected a sense of maturity and calm that made them different from the men around us, and it was their character, rather than their "monogamy," that struck me so. I recognized that their relationships were special in a significant way, although I couldn't yet specify what differentiated them from most others. I also knew that I wanted nothing less than that sort of relationship for myself. Observing their relationships led me to a

1

life-long interest in the subject that has since become the mainstay of my practice as a psychologist.

In graduate school, after the war, I came upon a study that made me think back to John and Steven. The study, conducted by Abraham Maslow, examined the lives of emotionally healthy people in an effort to learn what they had in common. One of Maslow's findings (which has since been published in Ashley Montagu's *The Practice of Love)* was that these people, whom he called "self-actualizing," all had ". . . love satisfactions and sex satisfactions that improved with the age of the relationship."

Think about it: a relationship that strengthens both sexually *and* emotionally over a long period of time. If the idea of such a relationship sounds impossible to you, consider yourself a victim of our culture. It's of little consolation to know that you are by no means alone, but the fact is that despite those few idealized relationships produced in Hollywood for the silver screen, most people today really believe that a romantic love that endures on both the physical and spiritual level is nothing but sentimental slop. After all, the divorce rates are there for us to look at. If we use them as our point of reference, we needn't even think about finding a deeply fulfilling and lasting love.

And if statistics aren't enough of an argument against the possibility of the type of relationships I saw in the Air Force (and have seen many times since), you can get further corroboration from most of my professional peers. Most of the literature in the field calls the belief in an enduring romantic-love relationship "delusional thinking." From Freud on down, social scientists have constructed what appears to be a rational thesis on the impossibility of long-term romantic and sexual fulfillment.

The tragedy of these various theses is that they have more to do with the personal problems of the people who wrote them than they do with romantic love. And, for a variety of reasons that we'll deal with later, we've all chosen to buy their problems! Years ago, when I first moved to Los Angeles, I read an article by an eminent psychoanalyst in which he talked about a middle-aged woman who had fallen madly in love. The therapist dis-

cussed this "phenomenon" as an adjunct of menopause
. . . a neurotic attempt to capture what she had missed in
her youth. The idea was that this woman was *clinically*
neurotic because she wanted a kind of happiness that was
somehow inappropriate to her stage of life.

I was incensed by the article. My personal viewpoint is
that you have one life and *only* one life, and it's your job
to find for yourself the greatest degree of serious, long-
range, deeply profound happiness. There is no age at
which the pursuit of that goal becomes inappropriate. I
frequently see middle-aged men and women who feel that
there's something wrong with them because they're pas-
sionately in love. If I personally felt that this sort of love
was essentially neurotic, I might pick up on my cues from
my patients and discuss hormonal imbalance during
menopause—rather than the issue of why they don't allow
themselves to feel good. I'd leave the session feeling safe,
and they'd leave it feeling empty.

Over the past thirty years my practice has been filled
with people of all ages who talk about a gnawing feeling
of emptiness. The emptiness frequently expresses itself as
depression, an epidemic of our times, and whenever we
get around to discussing love and romantic expectations, I
can easily understand the root of the depression—regardless
of how old the client is.

How can people feel anything but depressed when they
explain that they've been "happily" married for fifteen or
twenty years but almost never have sex with their husband
or wife? How can single people feel anything but depressed when they state, in a resigned tone of voice, that
the time has come for them to "settle down" and get
married, but when "settle down" has really become a
euphemism for "settling for less"? And how can anyone
feel anything but empty when they opt for a life with no
emotional "entanglements," when we all know that "entanglements" is a defensive way of saying "involvement"?

Rarely does a day go by that I don't hear someone talk
about a "fear of commitment." A young, dynamic, attractive woman I'm treating recently told me about a first date
that began with a total stranger telling her not to have any

expectations of him. I asked her how that made her feel and she said: "Angry. Lonely. What do I need this sort of thing for? After something like that I feel like I'd just as soon stay home." There are those among us who have been conditioned, in an almost Pavlovian way, to turn ourselves off if there's even the remote possibility of romantic involvement.

Of course, when I begin to talk to these people about the kind of relationship that's based on pleasure and that's charged with an enthusiasm that energizes still greater pleasure, they don't turn their thumbs down and say, "I don't want any part of that." Rather, they say things like, "Sure I want a man or a woman to be there for me the way you describe. There's just no one out there who even comes close." "How can I be expected to trust another man or woman after being dumped on so many times." "As soon as they know I care, they split." "All they want is sex/a mother/a father." "I feel so safe in *this* relationship. It doesn't seem worth risking something so safe if I don't have a guarantee of something better."

All of those voices, in one way or another, are saying that they find the prospect of a great, intense, enduring romantic love to be frightening. Whatever reasons you can give to explain the absence of this sort of relationship in your life—and such a relationship is indeed difficult to establish—the primary force that's keeping you from romantic-love fulfillment is submission to fear. Fear of intimacy, fear of loss, fear of making oneself vulnerable. Simply put, people need people to love and be loved by on two levels: spiritual and physical. Acknowledging our need for such a relationship can be a frightening prospect, but I know for a fact that denying that need is ultimately much more frightening.

Just as infants fail to thrive when they are deprived of holding and stroking, adults who do without the grown-up equivalent cannot truly approach their full potential to enjoy life. How many people do you know who spend twelve hours a day in an office for the first twenty years of a career before they begin to feel—in the form of a midlife crisis—a desperate sense of emptiness? How many people can you think of who invest so much passion and energy into their children that they just can't let go when the time comes for the kids to move on out? How about the people who, by the age of thirty-five, have a veneer so tough and so brittle that no one will even attempt to come close?

All of us are, to some extent, what I call amoro-phobics. Fortunately, like most phobias, amoro-phobia can be dealt with successfully. The real issue we need to grapple with is whether our phobia will control our life, or whether we will learn to control our phobia. The first step in dealing with our fear is understanding just what it is we're afraid of. Most people have a very misguided idea of what a healthy, vital romantic love is. In the first part of this book, just as in my many workshops, I will define the kind of relationships we have a right to want: a relationship that demands our full potential as individuals.

In Part II, I will discuss the issues of romantic phobia and vulnerability. Unless you can recognize the signals that mean you're shutting yourself in, you'll never be in a position to confront the issue. There are specific questions you can ask yourself before you close the door on a relationship that might, if given half an opportunity, help you to make it richer than you ever imagined. Other questions may help you summon up the courage to close a door that should have been shut years earlier.

In Part III, I will deal with the matter of making a relationship last. There's nothing especially rare about the first flush of romance. What makes intense romantic love, as I define it, so very, very precious is the fact that it can endure. If we were to experience romantic love throughout the life of the relationship in the same way we did very early on, no one would ever manage to get anything done! We have careers, families—a host of other things in our life that require attention and time—and a genuine romantic-love relationship allows room for it all. In fact, a genuine romantic-love relationship is the perfect incentive for encouraging growth in other areas of personal development.

My practice is composed of both men and women. The

problems people have forming intense romantic relationships are not limited to one sex. Men and women need romantic love; men and women are frightened by romantic love; and men and women frequently grapple with the same basic problems when they attempt to overcome their fears. Recognizing that the opposite sex is human and plagued by the same emotional burdens as you is an important step toward freeing yourself of those burdens.

For the sake of clarity of style, I have addressed my book to women, which means that when I talk about lovers I usually use "he" and "him". My choice was arbitrary and not meant to exclude men.

I'm by no means a sentimental man, but I do believe in both the pursuit and the attainment of happiness. The joy that goes along with a successful romantic-love relationship is exhilarating, and the fact that I'm close to that joy as frequently as I am is what makes my work so special. I know from personal experience, and from the experience of so many of the people I've worked with, that enduring, intense romantic love is a real possibility.

Unless you're willing to drop the facade of cynicism and allow yourself to believe in the possibility of a truly satisfying relationship, you'll never find one. This isn't Never-Never Land, and believing in things doesn't make them real, but *not* believing *does* make them seem impossible. While I never encourage people to work toward an impossible goal, I do encourage them to work toward difficult goals, particularly if I know that the payoff will make it all worthwhile.

PART I

Romantic Love:
WHAT IT'S ALL ABOUT

CHAPTER 1

What is Romantic Love

WHAT DO YOU THINK of when you hear the word "love"? Chances are that every person reading this book thinks of something different. "Love" is, to be sure, a broadly defined word that covers everything, from your feelings about parents, clothing, lovers, to your feelings about God. It might make matters easier if we had different words for different kinds of love, the way the Eskimos have different words for different kinds of snow. But since we don't, and since I want to address a very specific type of love, we'll need to begin with a definition.

Romantic love, as I define it, is the fusion of great spiritual affinity with intense sexual attraction. When those two components occur within a single relationship they elicit the most explosive, powerful, intense emotion of which human beings are capable. I am concerned with that intense, head-reeling, heart-pounding sort of love that lots of old movies attempted to portray, but ultimately distorted. The movies fell short of giving the total picture because they were concerned with providing entertainment, and life—and the relationships therein—is more complex than it is entertaining. But the movies (and the literature and songs) did succeed in fueling our imaginations and giving us the impression that we could all have the magic of great love. On some level, most of us believe that intense romantic love " could happen to us."

Yet most of us who are ardent believers in the phenomenon of intense romantic love have a hard time believing that these kinds of relationships can be enduring. And it's no wonder. Experts in the mental health field tell us that at best, the life span of romantic love as I define it—complete with intense sexual attraction and spiritual affinity—is thirty months. (A banner headline on the cover of *Reader's Digest* emphasized that a large percentage of couples who claim to be happily married report that they no longer have sex.) Many of these professionals suggest that the essence of emotional maturity involves letting go of our romantic expectations and replacing them with something more "realistic." Words like "companionship" and "compatability" are bandied about as representing a superior basis for a relationship than romantic love.

Yet romantic love, as I define it, requires the interaction of two absolutely mature people. Tapping your potential for a romantic relationship involves the kind of self-confidence, courage, and openness that only mature adults can muster. I am ardently opposed to any theory that suggests any connection between maturity and settling for a relationship that is less than a fulfilling romantic-love relationship. My work over the past thirty years has been to restore people's early faith in, and enthusiasm for enduring, intense romantic love, complete with bells ringing, waves crashing, and toes curling. I'm convinced that the emphasis that so many intellectuals place on "compatability," in place of romantic love, is largely responsible for much of the free-floating, nonspecific depression I see in my practice every day.

A successful, enduring romantic relationship means that two people get something from each other that they cannot get from any other person. It's important to note that such relationships do not fulfill all of our needs. No one person can be everything for someone else. We all *need* friends, confidantes, a variety of relationships, and a fulfilling work life to enrich our lives. But these other relationships don't fill the same emotional needs in the same way that

an intense romantic relationship does. They can't be sub-
stituted for each other.

Let's examine the two components of intense romantic
love more closely.

The Spirit

When I talk about "spiritual affinity" I don't mean
anything mystical. I use the words "spiritual" and "affinity" in much the way they're used in chemistry. In chemistry, "spirit" refers to the distilled essence of a substance.
"Affinity" means the attraction that one element has for
another.

A person's essence, or spirit, is that which makes one
totally unique. It incorporates one's deepest values, be-
liefs, convictions, and moral principles. Frequently this
inner core is covered by layers and layers of condition, but
the basis of deep friendship is getting beyond the external
layers and discovering a person's inner self. Once you feel
that you really understand another person's world-view,
you have a basis for trust; and without trust no relationship
of any sort is worth pursuing.

There is no fixed method for learning about what someone is like underneath all the layers he shows the outside
world. You can feel, on an intuitive level, like you know
someone after spending a very short time with him, or it
can take months or years for two people to unfold to each
other. In either case, it's the outcome that matters more
than the method or the clock. The important thing is that
you aren't taken in solely by appearances.

I treated a woman named Elaine who had a monumental
history of romantic disappointments. Finally, as she was
approaching her fortieth birthday she resolved *never* to go
out with a man unless there was a distinct obvious basis
for relating. Elaine was an advertising copywriter, a sports
enthusiast, fairly active in local politics, and clear on the
fact that she didn't want to have children.

After months of pressuring, a friend of hers finally
convinced her to "go out for a drink" with a man she

knew. He was a religious man, a widower with five children. He ran a family lumber business, and never did anything more strenuous than pick his eight-year-old daughter up and carry her on his shoulders.

Essentially, my patient agreed to meet John because she wanted to get her persistent friend off her back. When she came in for her session the next day she was absolutely glowing . . . if a bit tired. She explained:

"We got together at five . . . and you know how much I was dreading this whole thing. I figured a polite drink and home. Period. I'm not sure what happened. It was a drink, then dinner, then coffee . . . and we just went on for hours. I got home at about one. And I'm not even sure what it was we were talking about for so long. But it was so comfortable to be with him. What did we talk about? Let me think. Oh, I remember something that got us going. He dropped a spoon and did this weird little gesture . . . a superstitious kind of thing . . . that I remember my grandfather having done. It turns out that our families come from the same area of Wales and we talked about ancestry, family, superstition, and lots of nonsense. We talked about nothing that would sound very interesting if I were to repeat it . . . but it felt so right."

Based on what Elaine told me during that session about John it seemed evident that they liked each other; that they had the basis for a terrific *friendship*. The "spiritual affinity" aspect of an enduring romantic relationship is the same as that which provides the basis for deep friendship. And much as is the case with friendships, spiritual affinity frequently grows and takes on added dimensions with time.

But as I said earlier, spiritual affinity alone does not qualify a relationship as an intense romantic relationship. No matter how deep a friendship, it won't satisfy your need for romantic love unless it's accompanied by intense sexual attraction. Lots of people with significant friendships feel desperately lonely at their core.

The Flesh

The issue of sexuality in romantic relationships is much more complex and controversial than the issue of spiritual affinity. Romantic love is essentially sexual love. It's much more than sexual love, to be sure, but fundamentally and basically it is sexual. No relationship qualifies as an intense romantic relationship unless both people find each other to be extremely attractive sexually.

An intensely sexual relationship should transport you to the peak of physical pleasure. I can't describe for you what this pleasure peak should feel like, nor do I have any intention of attempting such a description. Sexual sensations are entirely individualized and personal. I must emphasize, however, that intense sexual satisfaction is something we each have a right, and a need, to pursue. This noble pursuit of pure pleasure is what makes a romantic relationship unique.

No relationship is intensely sexual if one person forgoes sexual fulfillment to please a lover. In an intensely sexual relationship the pleasure is mutual, but each person is involved with pursuing her own satisfaction. I don't mean to imply that in intense sexual relationships you shouldn't care about whether or not your lover is deriving pleasure. Most frequently partners in such a relationship will find it sexually gratifying to *give* pleasure. But such giving doesn't have its place in romantic love as I define it unless the giver is fulfilled as well. In an intensely sexual relationship each person is responsible for what she is feeling. Only you know whether or not you have reached the height of passion.

Psychological Aspects of Sex

A well-known sex therapist once commented, after re-reading the completed manuscript of a book she had written, that she was shocked to discover that the word "love" didn't appear once in her entire work. She said that she found the omission disturbing because she was certain that sex in the context of a loving relationship was much, much better than even the best sex outside of that context.

I was involved in some early work in sexual therapy—before Masters and Johnson came out with their famous study—and I discovered that it's often relatively easy to make people proficient lovers. Sexual technique can unquestionably be learned by anyone with an interest, or investment, in learning. But dealing with the issue of romantic love, and absorbing the impact that intense romantic love has on sexual relations, is considerably more complicated.

The impact of the psychological component on the sexual drive was never more clearly illustrated than in the case of Ray, a thirty-four-year-old veteran of the Vietnam War. Before Ray went to Vietnam he was an extremely physical young man. He played football in college, he was an all-round athlete, and he had an active sex life. He returned from the war paralyzed from the waist down. He could literally feel nothing.

Ray is a remarkable man, with great emotional strength, and he determined that he was going to have as full a life as he possibly could. He went on to law school and got his professional life in order. But he also knew that he would never be happy unless he had a fulfilling personal life as well. He was fortunate enough to meet a woman with whom he fell in love, who loved him in return. When I last spoke with Ray he was discussing their sexual relationship.

"I know this is going to sound kind of strange, since physically I can't feel a damn thing from the waist down, but I have an incredibly satisfying sex life . . . and Miranda feels the same way. I *feel* sexual. I feel a kind of sexual climax that's thoroughly satisfying when we make love. I don't feel any less satisfied by the sexual aspect of this relationship than I did in relationships before I was hit. I guess it's all psychological . . . in my head . . . but whatever it is, it feels just great!"

*   *   *

The psychological component of good sex is both complex and powerful. Ray's sexual fulfillment was entirely real in terms of his feelings and the impact it had on his life.

Attraction

Tastes vary as to what constitutes physical attractiveness. In the 1890s, heavy women were considered to be the epitome of sexiness; today the trend has gone to thinner body types. Some of us are drawn to tall, reedlike bodies, others to small, muscular physiques. Most women would be delighted to have Sophia Loren's bone structure. Most men would like to have Paul Newman's eyes. But mature adults with the capacity for intense romantic relationships know that extraordinary looks are not a prerequisite to romantic fulfillment. Classic, objective beauty does not always dictate "attractiveness."

A great deal of what we call attractiveness has to do with style and life experience. People develop their looks in much the way they develop a signature. We are all, to some extent, a work of art created by ourselves. The way we comb our hair, dress, or take care of our bodies, reflects our individuality, self-regard, and character. We respond to all of those things when we respond to the way a person looks.

The idea of responding emotionally to physical appearance— of attributing psychological traits to the way someone looks—is universal. One need only think of how we respond to a great piece of sculpture to verify such a reaction. When you look at Michelangelo's *David*, you respond emotionally to what you see, despite the fact that you know you are looking at a piece of stone. Surely if a piece of stone can elicit such a strong emotional reaction it's easy to understand why the way someone looks—strictly from a physical perspective—has the power to excite or repel us.

There's no reason to be apologetic about the emphasis you put on whether or not you find someone to be physically attractive. Physical attraction is crucial for an intense romantic relationship.

Lust

It is important to differentiate between the intensely sexual component of a romantic love relationship and lust. Lust is an intense sexual response that is not ultimately fulfilling for most people. It can feel good at times and fulfill certain needs, but you must be on guard to not confuse it with romantic love. Some sexually starved individuals might make that mistake.

In a lust-based relationship the focus is on possessing a person physically, on sexual release, and on physical satisfaction. Once you become satisfied physically in such a relationship—and that can be after several months, one evening, or perhaps a matter of minutes—there's no longer any desire to be with your lover. Hanging on to a lust relationship once the sexual interest has run out is guaranteed to leave you feeling terribly empty.

Alan, a twenty-five-year-old attorney, came to see me originally because he felt that he had developed a pattern of falling in love with "the wrong women." This is how he described his problem:

"I don't know what it is. I keep meeting these terrific women. They're exactly my type . . . small, sort of wiry looking . . . long hair . . . tiny waists . . . and built . . . you know what I mean? Maybe it sounds shallow, but I know what I like and I like women who look like that! Anyway, we'll go out, talk for a while, and both feel really turned on and head for my place where everything goes great. And I mean 'to the moon.' You know what I mean?

"The problem is that the next morning I just can't wait to get this person out of my apartment. It's not that she's done anything wrong . . . but I want her out. I don't understand it at all. I might see her again and again, but it's the same thing . . . this incredibly intense thing in bed, and perfectly fine the whole time we're leading up to sex, but after . . . I can't get away fast enough.''

It's interesting to note that sex in a lust relationship serves precisely the opposite function that sex does in an intensely romantic relationship. In relationships like Alan's, sexual satisfaction essentially saps the relationship of energy. In an enduring romantic relationship, sexual satisfaction energizes the relationship and keeps it going strong.

Putting It All Together

Great spiritual affinity, without intense sexual response, forms the basis of deep friendship. Intense sexual response without great spiritual affinity forms the basis of a lust response. But when great spiritual affinity and intense sexual response occur within one relationship, the result can be intense romantic love. And as I said earlier, there is nothing in the human experience that can generate greater life returns than the ecstasy that is romantic love.

For years I listened as some of my clients attempted to describe feelings they experienced in relationships that they considered successful. They talked about being overwhelmed while they were making love by a feeling of wholeness. One woman said that she felt as though every part of her—physical and emotional—was being touched at the same time. Another said that when she and her husband made love she once found herself crying. "There was something so enormous about it all," she attempted to explain. "I felt so totally embraced and embracing . . . I can't really explain it but it's enormously powerful."

The "wholeness" that these people were attempting to describe is the product of living in an intensely romantic-love relationship. This wholeness contrasts precisely with the free-floating depression and depleting emptiness that so many of my clients describe when they enter therapy.

Learning to develop the openness that allows for romantic love is no small task. As I said earlier, it requires all the maturity, insight, and emotional risk-taking you can gather to reach a point where you have even the basis for a romantic relationship. And once you establish a trusting spiritual relationship with the same person you find intensely sexually attractive you have just that—just the basis—of a romantic relationship.

Those two fundamentals are a starting point from which you can move on in a relationship. The energy that they engender, coupled with the ability to recognize your own problems and problems in the relationship, and the will to work on the problems, and an openness to learn *how* to work things through are all part of establishing an enduring romantic relationship.

The environment of a romantic-love relationship is an extraordinarily nurturing environment. The experience of involving your entire self in a relationship enables you to discover strengths you may never have been aware of. The trust implicit between two people in love enables them to resolve weaknesses that are too frightening to face alone.

Now that you understand precisely what I mean by romantic love you're in a position to work toward it in much the way my clients do in workshops, group, and individual therapy sessions. Throughout this book when I use the word "love" I mean nothing less than what I have described in this chapter.

CHAPTER 2

Authentic vs. Neurotic
Love

UP UNTIL THIS POINT I've emphasized the fact that an authentic romantic-love relationship can enrich your life in every possible way. A neurotic romantic-love relationship, however, is quite the reverse: it plays on the most insecure aspects of your personality and saps your energy. If you learn only one thing from this book, it should be how to differentiate between the two.

In much the way that we all have neurotic aspects to our personality, every relationship, no matter how healthy, will have its neurotic tendencies. The issue at hand is whether the neurotic aspects of your personality or the healthy ones will dominate. For the sake of clarity I'll establish a working definition of "neurotic."

Dr. Albert Ellis, in his excellent book *How to Live with a Neurotic*, says, "Neurosis is stupid behavior by a non-stupid person." Most frequently this "stupid" behavior is self-destructive. The basis of a neurotic relationship is formed by the neurotic's desire to achieve a sense of worthwhileness through the endorsement of another person. The sense of "worthwhileness" such a person seeks can be of the most obvious variety—marrying "up" socially—or considerably more subtle.

I once knew a man, the youngest of three brothers, who spent his life competing with his two very successful siblings. His brothers went to prestigious colleges and law schools, and so did he. His brothers each joined top-rate law firms, and so did he. When it came to women his pattern remained the same. He once told me during a session that he never really believed that he was very attractive to women, but that if he could get a "really terrific-looking" woman to go out with him he didn't feel like he was "too bad."

Both of his brothers were happily married to average-looking women. My client began dating a woman who was extraordinarily beautiful and came into a session one day feeling particularly good. He explained:

"Well, I asked Elana to marry me and she said yes. I tell you, I don't know when I've felt this good. Here I am with this gorgeous chick who wants to marry me. I must be a pretty sexy guy after all. And beside that, I finally got it over my brothers. I mean, my sisters-in-law are O.K., but I've obviously got the prize."

Why Love?

Remember an old song called "You're Nobody Till Somebody Loves You"? Well, forget it! That song title proclaims the very essence of neurotic love. Romantic love *cannot* make up for personal inadequacies. The issue of personal worth is strictly an internal psychological problem and has to be dealt with by each individual. If you're looking to a relationship for endorsement, validation, or escape from misery, you're heading for trouble.

Unfortunately it's not always easy to pick up on your own neurotic impulses. Lots of us don't even acknowledge that we are, in some part, neurotic . . . let alone admit that our own neurosis is at the root of a problem relationship. It's much easier to point a finger at someone else than it is to look inside. But after a while, pointing fingers becomes unsatisfying. That's when you should begin to ask yourself the following questions.

Why Would Someone Be Interested In Me?

Susan had been in therapy with me for only a short time when she met Bill. She was a legal secretary and he was an upcoming young lawyer in the firm for which she worked. This is how she described her feelings when he first asked her out.

"I couldn't believe it. I just couldn't believe that he was interested in me when there were so many other women in the firm . . . women lawyers even . . . that would have been thrilled to go out with him. I mean he's attractive, smart, and he's going to be very successful. I should check my horoscope or something. This must be my lucky day."

Despite Susan's proclamations, she must think Bill's a real jerk. Who but a jerk would give so much to get so little? After all, Bill is offering just about everything a man can offer, and Susan (according to her own evaluation) is there to get it because of nothing more than the position of her planets!

A relationship based on one person's gratitude for another person's attentions is doomed from both ends. Either the person in Bill's position will eventually resent the enormous burden of making Susan feel valuable, or the person in Susan's position will begin to feel suspicious and jealous of other women.

If your relationship is going to be authentic and healthy, you should be able to answer the question "Why would someone be interested in me?" quite easily, and the answer should have to do with your own real attributes. You're interesting, warm, attractive, caring, intelligent, challenging, and so on.

Who Is This Relationship For?

Ellen married her childhood sweetheart when she was nineteen and he was twenty-four. He was in his third year of medical school and she was finishing college. Both of their families were delighted with the match and in a financial position to help support the couple until they could make it on their own. They were what everyone called "a dynamic young couple," and everyone was shocked when they split up after ten years of marriage. Ellen explains:

"To this day I can't make my parents understand why Richard and I split up . . . but I've stopped trying. It's not that I didn't care for Richard as a person. He's a good person. I still believe that. It's just that we had no spark . . . no magic. He could almost have been my brother.

"Actually one of our biggest problems was that we were so involved with our families in the first place. Richard was a 'perfect' husband . . . from the point of view of my mother and father. I was so young when we got married that I never had much time to develop my own idea of what a perfect husband for me would be. The fact that his parents thought I was wonderful, and my parents were so happy was very, very important to me. I like my parents to be happy, and, no doubt about it, I *like* making *them* happy.

"But it knocks me out when I think about the degree of my sacrifice. It took me the full ten years of my marriage to admit to myself that something was missing. I was terrified to let go of the image other people had of me—of us, really—and I was even more terrified of how my parents would deal with our splitting up. For at least six months I thought that they would literally die when I told them that we were separating."

Needless to say, Ellen's parents didn't die. They were, to be sure, unhappy, but they coped with their disappointment a lot better than Ellen could have coped with a life-long commitment to an unsatisfying marriage. In the four years since her divorce Ellen has been able to separate her own needs from the needs of her family.

The idea of having a relationship for *other* people need not be restricted to family. You can't commit to another person because you think your friends will like him, or that he will be a good provider for your children. And you can't love someone because you think his feelings will be hurt if you reject him. Romantic love is *selfish*!

When it comes to an authentic romantic relationship, it is *your* pleasure, and *your* happiness that's the central base of emotion. Lots of people believe that real love is total selflessness and a generous concern for someone else is really at its root. As "nice" as this may sound, it has nothing to do with romantic love. A selfless romantic love is absurd. After all, what greater compliment can you pay a lover than to have him know that he is your greatest possible source of pleasure?

Ultimately a relationship is for the two people who comprise it. When you turn out the lights at night your mother/father/children/psychoanalyst/clergyman is not in bed with you. And if you're not happy with the face on the pillow next to yours, you're not going to have a full life together.

What Do I Want In A Partner?

Donald, a thirty-five-year-old real estate broker, came to see me because, unbeknownst to his wife of six years, he felt like his marriage was crumbling. He began his first session this way:

"When Simone and I first met I thought she was God's most perfect creation. I mean, she was beautiful, incredibly smart, she was a super-cook—maybe it's her French blood—and she had a really refined quality I'd never encountered before. She just seemed to know how to handle everything with grace. I can't really explain it any better than that. She was perfect. She was somewhere up there . . . I really had her on a pedestal.

"But in the last year something seems to have happened. It's almost as though every time I look at her I see another flaw. It's scaring the shit out of me. I swear that she's even begun to *smell* bad. Her nose looks big . . . it couldn't have grown? She doesn't have the patience with me that she once had, and she gets upset about all sorts of things.

"I know it doesn't make much sense, but I really feel like I'm watching her disintegrate. Frankly, my impulse is to run the hell away. She's not the woman I married."

Pedestals are terribly precarious perches. There is, simply, no room for them in romantic-love relationships. You can be sure that you're headed for a neurotic relationship if you think you've found perfection in a partner. There is no such animal as a perfect person.

If Donald had allowed Simone her "human-ness" before they got married, he would have had a much richer relationship with her. As it is, instead he had a relationship with his idea of her. Pedestals are like cages. The person on the inside can't really move around much and the person on the outside can't get close to his captive.

The Usual Mixture

I want to make it clear that I don't believe that anyone, and therefore any romantic relationship, is, or can be entirely free of neurotic components. Most people, and most relationships, combine a mixture of both neurotic and authentic elements. Any given relationship may go through periods during which it is more neurotic, and periods during which it is primarily authentic. But there is a difference between a relationship that sustains neurotic moods, and a neurotic relationship. The latter—as I said earlier—is based on the desire of one person to gain a sense of worth through her association with another.

The key to surviving periods during which neurotic moods dominate our romantic relationship lies in recognizing those feelings as neurotic, and learning how to minimize the negative impact of these neuroses on ourselves and on the relationship we value so highly. This game plan is a great deal more difficult to put into action than it is to discuss, but it can be done.

A couple once came to see me because the husband, Tony, felt their relationship was turning into a constant power struggle. Tony was a doctor, and his wife, Judith, had just finished applying to medical schools. She was waiting for a response and her entire sense of self-esteem seemed to be at stake each morning when she opened the mailbox. Tony felt that Judith, who had had a successful career in a different field before she decided to pursue a career in medicine, was jumping down his throat all the time.

"No matter what I say it seems to be wrong. If I try to assure her that she'll get into med school and be a great doctor, she tells me I don't understand how difficult it is these days and just because I got into a good medical school doesn't mean she will. If I tell her that she's right, it has gotten harder than it was ten years ago, she tells me I'm not supportive. She's always too tense for sex. She doesn't have time to really sit and talk because she's still taking pre-med courses. I don't know. I honestly felt very supportive of her career-change . . . and that's something, because I know what a grind she's got ahead of her and how little time she's going to have for me. But at this point I feel like she's already sacrificed the relationship . . . which is more important to me than anything."

Tony's great hope was that the current state of their relationship might be temporary, and that if Judith would accept some responsibility for her behavior their relationship would survive the tyranny of her neurosis. To the extent that Judith was willing to go to a therapist and discuss the problem, Tony had reason to be hopeful. In fact, Judith got into medical school and entered therapy and regained her equilibrium enough to appreciate the goodwill and support of her husband.

Problems You Never Knew About

In addition to struggling for enough objectivity in your relationship to determine where your problems begin and where they leave off, an intense, enduring romantic relationship may entail some unpleasant, but ultimately liberating surprises. Romantic intensity can bring neurotic problems out from under the rocks. At the very time that you become involved in the most fulfilling relationship of your life, you may also become aware of emotional problems you never knew existed.

This phenomenon is by no means uncommon, and when you stop to analyze it, it makes sense. An intensely romantic relationship creates an intimate atmosphere of trust and safety, in which both partners allow themselves to become extremely vulnerable. The openness that is integral to such a relationship implies looking *inside* yourself as much as it implies embracing someone else. This self-centered aspect of romantic love is not, by any means, bad news.

Becoming so aware of your problems makes it possible for someone who's invested in an important relationship to work effectively on improving himself and diminishing the effect of his neurotic problems. It's also a tribute to your courage, and a promising sign for the future of your relationship that you're able to open up to yourself. It means, at the very least, that you are willing to really trust another person to love you.

The Power of Neurotic Love

I want to emphasize here that I certainly acknowledge how difficult it is to remain aware of, and accept responsibility for your neurotic behavior. But consider the consequences. The more neurotic elements are indulged in a relationship, the less likely you are to find that relationship fulfilling. If you find yourself with someone who allows your neurotic impulses to go unchecked, in a very short time your relationship will actually become a dumping ground for the worst aspects of your personality.

Under such circumstances it's quite natural for whatever authentic love might have once existed to erode. This kind of erosion can happen so gradually that the damage may be irreparable by the time you discover the problem. Unfortunately, many people interpret the trust that's organic to a romantic-love relationship as license to treat their lovers carelessly.

There's not a damn thing romantic about "always hurting the one you love." The whole idea of taking your lover's feelings for granted is a terrible perversion of the love relationship. If there's anyone whose feelings you should be invested in protecting it makes sense for that person to be the one you love most in the world.

People in an enduring romantic-love relationship have great respect for each other, and that respect should be reflected in every aspect of the relationship. How do you talk to your lover? Unfortunately, it's not uncommon for people in a relationship to speak to each other with less respect than they might use in addressing a stranger. Think about it.

I once worked with a couple who felt that their relationship had somehow disintegrated without their knowledge. Rochelle felt, quite rightly, that David no longer treated her with respect. As a typical example she told me that they had been playing tennis the weekend before with some people they'd known for only a short time. Every time Rochelle missed a shot, David said something like, "I can't believe it. You've got to be a moron to miss that," or "How can you be such an idiot? You were supposed to be at the net for that."

I asked David if he really felt that Rochelle was a moron and an idiot and he said, "Of course not." I asked him what he thought would have happened if the couples decided to split teams and play with each other's spouses. Would he have spoken the same way to his friend's wife if she had missed the same shots? "Of course not," he said again, somewhat shocked by my suggestion. I pursued the point by asking him how he would have felt if he had been playing on the same side of the net with his friend, and if, every time he missed a shot, this friend called him a "moron."

David was quick to acknowledge that he would have felt very angry in such a situation. Indeed, he wouldn't have continued to play. Finally, when I asked him why he felt it was acceptable to treat Rochelle in a manner that would be insulting to anyone else . . . a manner in which he himself would not want to be treated, he could say nothing. He was silent, then shrugged his shoulders and whispered, "I guess I was nervous. We don't know these people very well and I was worried about what they'd think of us. I thought they'd find us less appealing because she was screwing up the game." He paused again. "I guess they found us less appealing because *I* was acting like such a jerk."

David had allowed his relationship to become the dumping ground for his social insecurities. Rather than talk to Rochelle about his anxiety beforehand, which in and of itself might have released some tension, he just projected his lousy self-image onto his wife. If his assumption was that she loved him "for better or for worse," he was right . . . but misguided. Loving for better or worse means accepting your lover's limitations. Rochelle would probably have continued to love David if he acknowledged his insecurities. Loving for better or for worse does not mean that you will accept abuse or neglect, regardless of what motivates that sort of behavior.

Enduring romantic love means always being willing to say you're sorry, and then examining the impulse that led you to exhibit such behavior. It's as damaging for you to speak disrespectfully to someone you love as it is to the relationship. Ultimately the kind of abuse that Rochelle experienced from David leads to guilt and the neurotic behavior guilt engenders.

You'll save yourself a great deal of heartache if you

approach romantic relationships with all the reason and objectivity you can muster. As I'll explain in the next chapter, such objectivity should not be confused with distance, or coldness.

CHAPTER 3

Objectivity, Reality,
and Authentic Love

Love, despite anything you've heard until now, should *never* be blind. Blind love is like a time bomb, set to go off as soon as reality sets in. Love based on realistic expectations, mutual acceptance, and understanding of the fact that both you and your lover have limitations, has a far better chance to endure. An effort to be realistic and objective in the beginning of a relationship will insure fewer unhappy surprises once you get rolling. And a genuine effort to really listen to what your lover is saying— even when it's something you don't like to hear—means that your channels of communication won't get bogged down in a power struggle.

In The Beginning

Where did the idea of blind love originate? Why are so many people—people who are prudent in every other sphere of their lives—myopic when it comes to forming their most important relationship? One explanation has to do with neediness. When you feel a sense of desperation about finding a romantic relationship, it's easy to want to overlook anything that appears to stand in the way . . . even when the very things you overlook will eventually contribute to its downfall. This sort of denial can come in the form of not seeing or hearing things that are clearly present, or of seeing them but saying, "It'll all change once we're married or living together or committed to each other."

Problems don't go away just because you want them to, and while certain things can change, others never will. It's not unreasonable for you to expect a lover to lose some weight, but there's no way anyone is going to grow three inches to make you happy. That analogy may sound absurd, but in one way or another many people enter relationships expecting changes as impossible as late-life growth spurts!

The Romantic Self-Protection Principle

The romantic self-protection principle is a safeguard against having our hopes define our reality. It states: *Never allow your romantic hopes to outdistance your reasonable expectations for success.* Memorize it. Write it on an index card, if you need to, and pull it out whenever you think you've met the "perfect person."

It's crucial to pay attention to any evidence—or lack of evidence of our romantic chances. Let's consider an analogy that has nothing to do with romance.

How hurt and disappointed are you that you're unable to own a large yacht or a private jet? Unless you're seriously disturbed (or very close, in terms of your personal finances, to owning these spectacular toys), you don't spend too much time suffering over their absence. If our expectations are reasonable and realistic, we need not suffer needlessly.

I'm not suggesting here that you lower your expectations in regard to a lover. I am suggesting that you measure your expectations realistically against the facts. This sort of measuring requires great vigilance. There's no room for selective hearing, selective vision, or the sort of magical thinking that says "wishing will make it so."

Basically, you should never compromise your feelings about your lover. You should feel—on a strictly gut emotional level—like you're in love. If you have that feeling, however, and you look at your lover and say, "But he's not six feet tall," or "She isn't younger than I am," you're interfering with an important emotional process.

A Case Of Selective Hearing

Consider Gwenn, a successful free-lance designer, and Myles, a stockbroker she met at Club Med almost two years ago. Gwenn was in her mid-thirties when she went to Club Med, and she was desperately eager to meet a man there. Myles had been living with a woman for close to ten years, and while they hadn't broken off their relationship, he viewed his solo trip to Club Med as a step in that direction.

Myles and Gwenn were instantly attracted to each other and spent their vacation together. At some point, near the time they were about to return home, he told Gwenn about Sandy—the woman at home. He said that he was still officially living with her, that he did, in fact, love her, but that he wasn't "in love" with her. Their relationship had become one of obligation and guilt. He also told Gwenn that he wanted to start looking for a place of his own, and that he hadn't had as wonderful a time with a woman for as long as he could remember. He really "loved being" with her.

At her first therapy session after her return from Club Med, Gwenn reported the following to me:

"This is the real thing, Roger. I went there letting myself hope for something. You always say that I need to believe in love before it can happen . . . and it really happened. Myles isn't like any man I've ever met. He's good to me, he actually told me that he *loved* me, and he's honest. That's the main thing. He's honest. I know about this thing with Sandy, and really can understand how difficult it is for him to break off with her after all these years. I mean, she was with him during some very hard times, and he has a lot of guilt about leaving her. But he's working on it. That's the thing. He's working on ending that relationship and freeing himself up for me. From my viewpoint, he's worth waiting for.''

Six months later Myles still hadn't broken off his relationship with Sandy, but he *had* intensified his relationship with Gwenn. According to Gwenn:

"Look, he spends every Thursday night and Friday night with her, but the rest of the week he's at my place. Most of his things—his clothing and records and stuff—are at my place. He doesn't even have sex with her, and our sex is . . . it's just spectacular. We spend hours making love.

"Still, it's getting a little hard on me. I don't want him to feel guilty about me the way he does about Sandy, but every now and then something happens and I feel like I want to force him into a decision. I know that's fucked-up of me, but certain things make me feel crazed. Like when his grandmother died last week I felt like I wanted to be with him and comfort him—he was close to his grandmother—but it turned out that Sandy did that. I guess because she's more like part of his family. It's not outrageous, but it made me feel very much on the periphery.

"But he's still the best thing that ever happened to me. No one has ever treated me so well. When he's with me, he's really *with* me. And the most important thing is that he still says that he loves me.''

In fact, Myles still said that he "loved being with" Gwenn. He also said that he still loved Sandy. Gwenn was right about Myles's honesty. She just couldn't hear the truth! When it suited her hopes, she heard more, and when what he said was painful, she heard less. They went on, in much the same manner, for nearly two years. Gwenn's periods of feeling "crazed" became more frequent, but

she still wouldn't acknowledge the difference between someone saying that they "loved being with" her, and someone
saying that they were "in love with" her. Ultimately, Myles
taught her to distinguish between the two. But until then
she insisted on seeing him as an angel caught in the trap of a
devil named Sandy. She absolved him of any responsibility.

Finally, after two years, Gwenn's selective hearing was
forced to an end. Myles put an end to it. By this time he
had found an apartment of his own and really ended things
with Sandy. Unfortunately for Gwenn, whom he still "loved
being with," he had met a third woman with whom he was
head-over-heels "in love." Gwenn described their last time
together this way:

"He said that he still wanted to see me because I was a
terrific woman and that he still loved being with me. But
he was really in love with this other woman. He'd never
known love could be so . . . so intense. The thing that
kills me is that he told me he would never have been able
to end his relationship with Sandy without my support and
help. God! How could I have been such a jerk?"

Gwenn is not a jerk. She just allowed her neediness to
obscure her vision. She explained away the selfless quality
of her relationship with Myles by comparing it to past
relationships that were even more deficient. It may well be
that no other man had ever been so good to her, but she
still has a right to more than that. Her sense of desperation
led her to feel grateful for crumbs, rather than eager for the
whole cake. She was primed for a disappointing relationship because she cared more about being in a relationship
than she did about taking care of herself.

The Restaurant Principle

I don't believe people ever want to get hurt in relationships. I've seen people, like Gwenn, who are stupidly hurt
all the time and remain in excruciating circumstances; but
when I talk with them it's evident that they don't want to

be in emotional pain. They want happiness, but they don't know how to go about finding it. From the outside, a person's romantic history may make her look like a masochist, but when you get inside, the cause of all the hurt is usually ignorance, fear, stupidity, irrationality, and a desperate desire to be loved by someone. Many people who feel essentially worthless assume that when someone comes along and treats them as though they're without value they are only getting what they deserve.

I once had a client who spent years with a man who treated her abominably. Whenever I asked her why she put up with such poor treatment she would say, "But I love him." From this client was born my "restaurant principle."

Imagine an incredible restaurant: the décor is spectacular; the service is impeccable; the prices are within reason; and the food is better than you've ever tasted elsewhere. The only hitch is that every time you get home from this place you become deathly ill.

After a while—one hopes a short while—you have to ask yourself how long you will continue to frequent this restaurant. If you're rational, you'll make the decision to give up this "nearly" perfect dining experience. The same type of rational thought should go into determining what path to take in your romantic life.

Angels and Devils

The issue of putting people on pedestals—which I touched on earlier—is exceptionally important in the establishment of a solid love relationship. Objectivity about our own strengths and weaknesses and those of our partner is at the foundation of authentic romantic love. No one is without limitations. That simple fact is another thing you might need to write out on an index card and carry around with you for a while. People are, by definition, limited. It's easy to keep the idea of limitations in mind before you get embroiled in a love affair, but it's more difficult to maintain that degree of reason when the heat's on.

Essentially, we should never look to one person to take

care of all of our needs. We need a network of caring people to turn to when our romantic partner can't help us; and we have to be confident enough about our spiritual affinity—about the fact that we are drawn to our lover in a way that we aren't drawn to anyone else—to accept his limitations.

We've all heard people say, "I want to be loved for who I am." Although the concept behind that statement is frequently used to escape self-examination—as in the case of an obese person who refuses to lose weight because she wants "to be loved for who I am, not for how I look" —there's just no such thing as an authentic romantic love that doesn't allow room for limitations.

Just how many limitations, and what kinds of limitations you're willing to accept will vary, of course, in the context of a relationship. It's not terribly difficult for a woman to accept the fact that the great love of her life simply cannot tolerate shopping for clothing, and that she can't expect him to accompany her on shopping forays. Actually, our culture is inclined to support that sort of limitation in a man, just as it supports the idea that a woman may not want to spend all day Sunday watching football games. These situations are as clichéd as coping with a mate who squeezes the toothpaste tube from the middle, rather than from the end. They're easy to deal with.

Things get tougher, however, when we move away from cartoon limitations and into the complex area of human character. Consider the situation of Judy and Ian. Judy is an extremely outgoing person with a great deal of social ease and grace. Ian is a very private person who hates the idea of big parties and meeting lots of new people. Judy and Ian don't question for a minute that they are very much in love with each other, but initially they had a great deal of adjusting to do in order to accommodate each other's concept of "socializing."

Early on in their relationship, Judy, who was in treatment with me, frequently felt pangs of being "unloved" by Ian because he didn't want to go partying with her. He never objected to her going to a party by herself, but he made the effort once or twice to join her and had an absolutely awful time. She tried staying home and found herself feeling resentful.

Fortunately, the core of their relationship was strong enough so that they never lost sight of how very special they each regarded their relationship as being. They managed, despite an occasional slip, to avoid personalizing their differences and turning them into power struggles, because they respected each other's preference. They also held on to a belief that if it were very important to one, or another of them, they would make an effort to extend themselves. Judy described one such situation:

"I know how much Ian hates big gatherings, and I try really hard not to put him in situations where he won't feel comfortable, but a few months ago I left my job and the people in my office threw a big farewell bash for me. It wasn't a surprise or anything, and I was both happy and tense as soon as they told me what they were doing. The first thing I thought was, 'I want Ian to be there and he just won't go.'

"Sure enough, when I got home I told Ian what they were doing and he gave his usual bit about hating parties and that he'd go out to dinner with a few friends, but he couldn't hack a big scene—the usual thing he says when I broach the subject. The thing is, this time I really felt like crying. After all the time we'd been together, I *still* felt like crying. My first, gut impulse was to say, 'If you loved me you would come.'

"But instead of giving in to that impulse I stopped myself for a moment. I *know* that Ian loves me. What I really was feeling was that this was a special situation and more important to me than others. Instead of feeling all hurt and unloved I was able to talk to him about how good it made me feel that people I'd spent three years working with were throwing a party in my honor, and how important it was *in this particular case* for Ian to be there with me

"Sure enough, he came. The thing is that he was able to hear me, just as I was able to talk to him . . . instead of our having a fight and confusing the issue with whether or not we love each other. We really work hard at listening. If, after I talked to Ian he still said he couldn't go to this party, I'd like to think that I would accept his decision, although I must admit that it would have been really hard. I'd have to believe, though, that he wants to make me happy, and will always try his best. Sometimes his best isn't all I'd hope it would be, but I still love him.''

It's Not The Cupcakes

Being able to check a neurotic reaction before you act on it, as Judy did with her feeling that Ian didn't love her, is no easy task. It requires a great deal of trust, insight, and, in a sense, discipline. One couple I worked with actually developed a "technique" to keep themselves on track when they felt like they were slipping into the realms of irrationality. The technique hinged on the verbal alarm: "It's not the cupcakes."

Early on in their relationship they had decided to spend a Sunday baking—something they both liked to do. As they were getting the ingredients ready the phone rang and Eleanor spent a half hour or so chatting with her best friend. After she hung up she and Joe resumed their activity, but Eleanor noticed that the whole tone of the day seemed different.

Somehow the first batch of cupcakes to come out of the oven was a total disaster. They were flat, burned, heavy . . . everything that could possibly be wrong with a cupcake was wrong with these cupcakes. And Joe flew off the handle. He spent a good ten minutes ranting and raving and berating Eleanor about how she had ruined his day and "didn't give a damn about his feelings and the cupcakes."

Eleanor, needless to say, was totally at a loss. She fought back her impulse to respond to Joe's hysteria with her own hysteria and waited until she thought he was finished with his tirade. Finally she managed to say, "What the hell is wrong? It's not the cupcakes."

Again he went on about the cupcakes. "They would

have been terrific if you had cared enough to watch them. I can't do it myself. . . ." And again Eleanor said, "It's not the cupcakes." Finally, after a few rounds of this, Joe calmed down. The whole scene sounds almost comic in the telling, but he was obviously upset, and Eleanor had no idea where all the intensity was coming from. She did know, for sure, that it wasn't because they had ruined a batch of cupcakes.

After Joe regained his sanity they talked. It turned out that he had seen this day as an intimate time together and had, in fact, been feeling neglected by Eleanor who spent a great deal of time with her many women friends. The phone call that postponed their activity was the last straw, and the burned cupcakes were evidence of her neglect.

If Eleanor hadn't had a strong enough base in her relationship with Joe, their fight might have become mired in the issue of the cupcakes. Stranger things happen every day. Because they have a real romantic love, they usually manage to avoid getting stuck in nonessentials. But they use a code now. When they begin to feel something brewing one of them will say, "It's not the cupcakes," and they both stop to listen.

CHAPTER 4

Conditional Love

ONE OF THE HARDEST FACTS to face about a healthy, vital romantic relationship is that it doesn't come with a guarantee. Romantic love is *always* conditional. It's voluntary and mutual, or it's not valid. You simply cannot coerce or legislate emotions. Two people should remain together only for as long as they *both* desire being together.

Somehow, despite the harsh reality of today's divorce statistics, the promise of "till death do us part" still carries enormous weight on the security front. We've all got that little bit of child in us that says, "I want someone to love me no matter what I do, no matter what I say, no matter how I look and no matter what I believe." Unfortunately, that child's voice gets in the way of intense romantic love.

Guaranteed Love

It's appropriate for a parent to love a child unconditionally. Children feel safe because of the unconditional nature of their parents' love. They know that they can always come home to be held and reinforced before they venture back into a world full of bumps and bruises and strangers.

But think for a moment of all the divorced men and women you know who explain the dissolution of their marriage by saying, "I realize that I was married to my father and that's not what I want."

I'm certain that one reason people marry "their father" is that they want to create the illusion of security that they associate with parental love. Actually, security in an intense romantic relationship is fragile and stems more from an appreciation of your partner as a totally unique individual than it does from a promise you made on your wedding day.

Romantic Love Decline

I have already talked about how easily romantic love can slip away, and how important it is to protect your romantic relationship if you expect it to survive. One important way of protecting your relationship that I've discussed involves treating your lover with the utmost respect.

Another important safeguard for your relationship requires that you *always* allow adequate time for the relationship. Arlene and Howard are a fairly typical case of a couple that didn't put the demands of their relationship above other things. They lost sight of the fact that an enduring romantic relationship was, in fact, the most valuable thing they could have.

Arlene and Howard came to me when they could no longer deny the fact that their marriage of twenty-five years was crumbling. They were both miserable and had been for some time before Howard got involved with a woman from his office; but it was only after he fell in love with this woman, Donna, that he was able to contrast an intensely romantic relationship with what his marriage had become.

"When Arlene and I first started dating we were both kids. And we were really in love with each other. The idea of seeing her would make me excited. There were always things to talk about . . . things to share. I lived in a different town from her and I—I should say 'we' because I know she felt the same—lived for weekends and the time we were together.

"But somehow, a few years after we got married everything seemed to change. Maybe we began to take each other for granted. I guess all married couples do that. I don't know. I only know that we were always too busy with things—friends, the house, and then the kids and everything that comes with them—to take time for just the two of us. Even the way we talked to each other changed. All we ever talked about was what needed to be done to keep things running smoothly. Everything was business and after a while I really began to feel empty.

"Maybe I'm stupid, but I just don't want my life to be that way anymore. Until I got involved with Donna—and believe me I felt plenty of guilt about that—I'd forgotten that I could enjoy being with a woman this way. I still care about Arlene, but I want more in my life. Somewhere along the line we stopped being in love."

Shortly after Arlene and Howard split up they both did amazingly similar things. They both went on diets and began exercising. They both started buying new wardrobes. In fact, six months after their separation they each looked more like their wedding picture than like a picture taken of them a year before the separation. And despite the fact that Arlene thought she'd never survive on her own, she found herself a job and admitted to feeling better about herself and her abilities than she had in years.

Enduring romantic love is an exceptionally fragile phenomenon and unless it's valued, above all else, it doesn't have much chance of surviving. One couple I worked with decided that they would set aside one weekend every month to be with each other. On that weekend they didn't make any dates with friends or even go to the movies. On Saturday evening they made a gourmet dinner for themselves, ate it by candlelight, put on their telephone answering machine, opened a good bottle of champagne, listened to music and made love . . . very leisurely. They viewed this weekend as their defense against the pressures of their life intruding on their relationship, which was, for both of them, a haven. Rather than allocate "left-over time" to their relationship—i.e., whatever was left after work, friends, family—they decided it was worth prime time. Had Arlene and Howard made such a decision early on, their romantic love might not have been subject to such extreme decline.

Appreciation Decline

It's essential to differentiate between *romantic-love decline* and *appreciation decline*. The couple I just described who took time out to appreciate their relationship were actually guarding against the possibility of appreciation decline. When I was in the South Pacific during World War II we had to live without a lot of life's luxuries. By "luxury" I mean such things as hot water, fresh eggs, meat. I remember thinking that if I ever got back to the States I would never again take a hot shower without pausing for a moment to think about how fortunate I was.

I've got to admit that I've taken thousands of showers since my return without pause. Fresh eggs don't mean anything very special to me anymore. Occasionally, when I go camping, I develop a new appreciation for indoor plumbing, but even that appreciation doesn't last long after my return to civilization. The things I've just described are no less valuable because I have them. The difference is that now I take them for granted.

Decline of appreciation, in the sense I've just described, doesn't really cause any great damage. If not understood, decline of appreciation, as it applies to a relationship, however, is potentially disastrous, and it is one of the pitfalls of unconditional love. When you have a long-term relationship with someone, you simply cannot take it for granted. If you make an effort to appreciate what you've got—by allocating time for it, by always seeing your lover as an individual worthy of respect—then you will appreciate it.

I know that when either my wife or I have to go away alone on some business or family matter, there's something exciting about our reunion. When we get back together our appreciation of each other and the relationship we have is at a peak. It always demonstrates to me that there's much, much more there in our relationship, in terms of pleasure and the level of happiness we give each other, than we are aware of in our day-in, day-out existence. Most of the great value is just taken for granted.

Frequently a couple will come to see me because they think the level of romantic love in their relationship is declining. After we talk awhile I can ascertain that they still love each other very much, but that they have stopped appreciating the enormous value of their relationship. One method of renewing their appreciation involves a series of "Think-Back Exercises."

Think-Back Exercises involve setting aside a special time to be with your lover—a time safe from intrusion and petty interruption, and talking to each other about the early stages of your relationship. If you have an enduring, intense romantic relationship, those early years will be a treasure that you share. Talking about them together is an extraordinarily effective way to evoke the most special qualities of your relationship.

I recommend that these "Think-Back Exercises" cover all sorts of specifics: the day you met and your first thoughts about each other; the first time you were alone with each other (a date or an office lunch); the first time you made love, and the events that led up to it; the first time you told someone else (a good friend) that you were in love; the first time you met each other's families; the day your first child was born; a big fight you had and how it was resolved.

If you still have an intense romantic relationship, these exercises will help renew your appreciation of it by reminding you just how it came to be. If you "think-back" and come up with sheer sentimentality, as opposed to a genuine renewal of feeling, then your problem may not have to do with appreciation decline so much as decline in romantic love.

Separateness

Many years ago when a famous theatrical couple split up, the woman told an interviewer that one of their problems was that their identities had merged. That they had come to know each other so well that being together felt like being alone. She said that when she reached out and took his hand, she might just as well have been holding her own. The consequences of this kind of merging on a couple's sex life is, obviously, disastrous.

Very often intimacy is lost between two people because of familiarity. If you keep in mind that your spouse is another person—a separate human being—and that no matter how well you know him and his likes and dislikes you can't ever really totally know a separate person, you'll never have to worry about a total merging. The more real that separateness remains in your mind, the easier it will be to maintain interest. Enduring romantic love thrives on the ability we have to surprise our mate, either with our feelings, our knowledge, our ignorance (of some things), or our desires. If you get to the point where making love with your spouse might just as well be masturbation, it's time for you to renew your distance. You'll never again be strangers across a crowded room, but there's no reason why you can't underscore the unknown.

Individuality

Individuality is a different issue from separateness, although the two are related. The most important condition upon which enduring, intense romantic love rests is that you maintain your individuality in a relationship. After all, it's the individual that you fell in love with in the first place!

The only way you can maintain your individuality is to find someone who loves you specifically because you are who you are. There is presently no scientific process for developing that sort of relationship; it just happens. You may be out with someone who has a habit that other people might find annoying, but for some reason makes a touching little dent on your heart. It's all of those touching little dents—all the idiosyncrasies of personality that add up to unique individuality. And an appreciation of your lover as a unique individual is the only real guard against decline of appreciation.

At a workshop I conducted a few years ago a young woman named Diana contrasted her current relationship with a string of other, less-satisfying relationships she'd had:

"A few years ago I went camping with a friend of mine, her husband, and her husband's best friend. We were staying at campgrounds near a really charming town in western Massachusetts and at some point during the first afternoon we decided to go into town. The best part of this town was the bookstore . . . it had couches and chairs and fresh fruit and cider and, of course, an incredible selection of books. It was really the type of bookstore you could curl up and spend the day in.

"We all went in and I started looking around, and about five minutes after we walked through the door the three of them were ready to leave. I suggested that they move on in the town and we meet in about a half hour at a lunch place and they thought I was nuts. They spent the rest of the weekend making fun of me because I was more interested in digging around in the bookstore than in doing whatever it was they wanted to do.

"When Allen and I got involved I remember telling him about that weekend. It was really upsetting to me. Basically I wasn't secure enough to feel good about what I wanted to do. I kept thinking that I should be more like them. Allen responded by saying that they sounded like a bunch of creeps, and by asking lots of questions about this incredible bookstore, which was what interested him. Maybe because Allen's whole orientation is so much like mine I feel comfortable being myself with him. In fact, the more I just relax and act instinctually when I'm with Allen, the closer we feel to each other.''

The important issue that Diana's experience illustrates is not whether or not it's better to spend your time in bookstores than elsewhere; but that it's crucial to find a romantic partner that responds to you and shares a basic sense of values with you. I'm not very big on the issue of compatibility, but I do believe that there has to be a basic, gut connection between two people if they're going to click in a relationship. If someone doesn't respond positively to the things that excite you—or at the very least, if someone doesn't appreciate your right to have your own interests— it's easy to get caught in a relationship where one person is busy trying to change the other, or where you feel like you have to change yourself to keep up the level of appreciation.

Diana went on to discuss how secure she felt about her new relationship. When another participant in the workshop asked about when she was going to get married, she said she really hadn't thought about it. She paused for a moment to reflect and added that her relationship with Allen was the first she'd ever been in where marriage and commitment weren't constantly on her mind. Six months after the workshop Diana wrote me a note saying that she and Allen had been married.

Risk-taking and Romance

There's a line in *Zorba the Greek* in which Zorba says, "Life *is* trouble. Only death is not." You know you're alive because you can feel things emotionally, and those feelings run the gamut from joy to pain. Zorba's statement can easily be extended to explain the nature of risk-taking and romantic love.

Romantic love is risky. It requires emotional risks of the highest order. Rejection in the romantic realm can be devastating, but an unwillingness to risk that devastation is guaranteed to be disastrous. If we're not willing to take risks, we have to settle for less fulfillment in life, and that's ultimately worse than the pain of rejection. In addition, people who are unwilling to take risks for romantic love feel a generalized emptiness, but they don't really know what it *is* that they're missing. They don't know that they're unwilling to take risks!

The ideal is to be willing to take risks that are reasonable—not *safe*, but reasonable. The process of what I've come to call "Mature Risk-taking," as it applies to forming relationships, is something I'll deal with in greater detail later. That love is conditional also means that the initial risk you take when you first form a relationship is, to some degree, always there. Commitment to a relationship doesn't and shouldn't mean that there's no longer any emotional risk. Quite the contrary. The more you love someone, the deeper the commitment, and the more vulnerable you are to the possibility of losing that love.

Is It Just For The Moment We Live?

By now you may be asking yourself, "Why bother?" If it's all so shaky, can it be worthwhile? Actually, romantic love isn't really shaky. It's certainly no more shaky than life itself. Somehow or other we all learn to cope with the fact of our mortality. We all know that we're eventually going to die, but we don't spend our days sitting in a dark room contemplating the end.

Rather, the idea of our own mortality is often the spur for new activity. There's often a feeling of grabbing all that life has to offer while you can, and of living to the hilt. Any fool can die, but not everyone can apply her talents and energies to living the most fulfilling life possible. Living "properly" is an art and a skill which can be learned.

I've learned, in my many years of practicing psychotherapy, that couples who appreciate the conditional quality of romantic love usually have a greater appreciation of every aspect of their relationship. They seem always to be discovering new things about their lover and bringing new energy into their relationship, in much the way a person who's had a close brush with death might develop a new enthusiasm for life.

Kira, a twenty-eight-year-old woman, first married when she was only nineteen years old. That marriage lasted three years and she began therapy shortly after her divorce. A year later she met a man through her work and they fell in love. She discussed some of the differences between her first and second marriage in a session with me not too long ago:

"When John and I got married we were both more excited with the idea of being married than we were with each other. I remember thinking how lucky I was to be *married* . . . not how lucky I was to have *John* as a part of my life. It's not that he wasn't a good person, or anything like that. It's just that I wanted to be married and have babies and do that whole trip.

"Thank God we didn't have any kids. We both knew there was something missing because we felt kind of empty. Dick and I started out in an entirely different way. We were both working on a magazine. I was just beginning to feel independent and good about myself. The last thing I was thinking about was finding another husband. But the first time I heard Dick discussing an article idea I remember thinking, 'This guy really sees things in an interesting way.' He felt the same way, and to this day we seem to have a constant flow of ideas between us. I mean, Dick is interested in me because of who I am . . . what makes me *different* from other people . . . not because he wants a wife and all the accoutrements of married life.

"On the one hand I feel like our relationship is based on the idea of us both always growing and learning and thinking, and that's a little scary. I can't be lazy about myself. On the other hand I feel like the premise of our relationship makes us more *secure* because there's so much mutual respect."

Kira discovered that conditional love is actually a great deal *more* secure than unconditional love; that having some-

one love you precisely *because* of what you say and think
and believe is more secure than having someone love you
despite what you say and think and believe. A wife or a
husband is replaceable, but Kira and Dick, as totally unique
individuals, are not.

Of course, before you can feel the security of a relationship that's based on the meeting of two complete individuals, you have to feel a good deal of self-confidence. You
have to feel that you have something special to offer
someone. The less secure you feel about yourself, the
more you're going to want guarantees, no matter how
unrealistic those guarantees are.

Sexual Self-Confidence

I've seen lots of people, both men and women, who
cling to an otherwise unsatisfying relationship because it
provides regular and satisfying sex. One of my clients was
married to a man for ten years and came to see me because
she was depressed. For a long time she denied that her
depression had anything to do with problems in her marriage. She was insistent on the issue of how much she
loved her husband and how, despite the fact that he occasionally had affairs with other women and that he had
physically abused her on three different occasions, he also
loved her.

Slowly she began to uncover her anger, but even then
she wasn't able to think about ending her marriage:

"I think he probably married me so that my father
would take him into the family business. Since Daddy
died, two years ago, things seem to have gotten worse
between us. I feel like he flaunts his affairs and almost
enjoys humiliating me. But I can't help loving him. I don't
know why I love him, but I do."

When she talked about their sex life her face lit up.

"He's most loving when we go to bed. He's really a terrific lover. No one could make me feel the way he does. I can't imagine going to bed with another man. It just couldn't be as good."

At some point I asked her if she thought she had any part in making their sex life so good, and she looked at me as though the thought had never occurred to her. I kept driving home the idea that she was at least fifty percent responsible for the good time they had in bed, and that if she were a good lover with her husband, who treated her so poorly, she'd be just as good a lover with a man who treated her well.

As soon as she began to assume some responsibility for the good part of her marriage—the sex—she began to feel less needy of her husband. Eventually she began to discern between feeling like she *needed* her husband (to feel desirable) and feeling like she *loved* her husband. The distinction was very important for her. When she accepted the fact that she had something that she was offering she felt less willing to be humiliated and abused. After all, if they split up, which they eventually did, she would be able to bring her passion elsewhere, where it could be appreciated.

Commitment

Where does commitment fit in with conditional love? You picked up this book hoping to learn how to make relationships endure, and I keep emphasizing the fact that there's no safe guarantee in love. I'm going to add to your confusion by saying that I think marriage is a great institution, and I think commitment is the natural outcome of intense romantic love.

The key to understanding romantic commitment and the essence of marriage as I think it should be, is to differentiate between commitment of *intent* and guarantees. Consider the case of Sivan, a thirty-three-year-old woman who left her husband, on friendly terms, because their marriage wasn't sexually satisfying to either of them. Sivan began to go out with other men and, much to her delight discovered that she was able to have a good time in bed. As her sexual confidence began to build she began to want more emotionally from her partners. She wanted a committed relationship.

This is how she went about it:

"As far as I'm concerned, there just aren't any men left who are willing to make a commitment. I'm ready, and God knows I'm willing. It's at a point now where when I meet a guy I tell him straight off that I'm looking for a serious relationship, that I'm too old to be screwing around, and that if he can't honestly tell me that he's interested in the same thing, we should call it off before it starts. That way neither one of us has to get hurt.

"Nine times out of ten that's the end of the affair. Some guys will make promises like, 'I think I want to spend my life with you' but I'm not going to bank on anything so flimsy. As soon as I get really serious, most men just disappear."

The biggest mistake Sivan is making has to do with wanting something that's impossible to give. There's simply no such thing as an iron-clad romantic guarantee. Later, when I talk about phobias, we'll discuss the pursuit of that kind of guarantee as a method of *avoiding* romantic involvement. Right now it's enough to say that Sivan is pursuing an impossible dream.

Essentially Sivan wants someone else to make her feel secure, and it just won't happen. She's so terrified of getting hurt that she's asking for commitments from total strangers. How can a man or woman think about a commitment except in the context of a relationship? If she's not willing to build up to a commitment with an investment of time and emotional vulnerability, why should anyone promise anything? Commitment in the context of an enduring, intense romantic relationship must never, never be confused with any sort of trap.

Many people are afraid of romantic commitment because they equate it with "getting stuck." This fear is especially intense in people who have had bad experiences in relationships and had a hard time extricating themselves. When, finally, they do break loose from their unhappy relationship, they often feel that they can no longer trust their judgment, and that if they make a mistake again, they'll never get out. It's ironic that people with this sort of fear usually say that they're afraid to trust *others*, when, in fact, they're terrified of trusting themselves.

Until these people begin to trust themselves, they'll never have the freedom to make a commitment to the kind of relationship that delivers the most serious and profound kind of pleasure imaginable. The first step toward self-trust, in this situation, is coming to understand the nature of conditional love. If a voice deep inside you is saying, "Don't commit," it's entirely possible that this inner voice is telling you something about the intensity of your feelings. Fear of commitment may be because there just isn't as much intense love as there should be. In that case your fear of getting stuck is entirely reasonable and realistic. Inherent in the concept of conditional love is the idea that commitment is *never* coerced.

There's a delicate line we must learn to draw that differentiates a proper heeding of one's fear from the possible occurrence of romantic phobia. You can make an error in either direction: you can pay too much attention to your fears and apprehensions; or can pay no attention to perfectly appropriate, healthy fears. After the emotion of fear is identified, the basis of your fear must be analyzed. If you're afraid of being deeply hurt by the possibility of rejection by, or loss of a person, you can assume that a phobia is rearing its ugly head. If, however, you're just not very happy, and suspect that your lover doesn't really "do it" for you, your fear is probably relevant.

Commitment Of Intent

The only kind of commitment that one can make if she understands the conditional nature of intense romantic love is "commitment of intent." Commitment of intent means simply that our every *intent*ion at the time of our commitment is to follow it to the letter. Usually, a healthy commitment of intent develops in stages.

The first degree of intent comes when a couple are dating occasionally. That's one degree in a relationship. If that kind of relationship is mutually pleasurable, the next natural step is to begin dating exclusively. This step marks another degree of intent. From there a couple might chose to live together. Finally, the highest degree of intent of commitment involves marriage—a formalized announcement to the world that they intend to continue loving each other indefinitely.

When people get married it is their *intent* to remain together forever. We don't get married with the idea that we're going to get divorced. Clearly, the expression "Till death do us part" has no place in a commitment of intent. I feel more comfortable with "As long as we both shall love," but that promise makes many people feel insecure. The insecurity that this promise evokes is a reflection of our inability to accept the conditional quality of adult love.

Divorce statistics bear out the fact that promises of "Till death do us part" have become somewhat meaningless. The freedom that comes with accepting that your relationship is, and always will be based on mutual, voluntary love, is actually a much more secure guarantee of a lifelong relationship. We need to view relationships in the same way we view mortality. We're all going to die someday, but we don't go around brooding about our mortality. In fact many of us appreciate life much more because we accept our own eventual deaths. The fact that relationships don't come with iron-clad guarantees should add to, rather than detract from our appreciation of them.

A Marriage Ceremony

The following marriage ceremony is a good expression of what Amy and David felt, and how they saw their future. It is clearly a ceremony based on commitment of intent, yet we come away from it feeling sec\ 56

what the years will bring them.

INTRODUCTION

Amy and David have honored us by inviting us to be with them during this time in which they will become husband and wife. Although what they mean to each other is apparent in their lives, it is less easily expressed in the language of a ceremony.

The ceremony which we are about to perform will not unite you in marriage. Only you can do that. The union that you are about to publicly formalize is not a casual one and not to be taken lightly, but the most important into which you will ever enter. If the relationship between two people, which is symbolized in our culture by the state of marriage, does not already exist between you, this ceremony will not create it. This ceremony is simply the public announcement of the existence of that relationship. The state, the church, or any other agency can only give its recognition to the bond between you. The state of marriage can exist between two people only when they wish it to exist and it does at that moment come to be. As you give public announcement to the existence of the bond uniting you by means of this ceremony which you are about to perform, keep in mind that you, together, have created this marriage.

You must never forget that you are each individuals and that there can only be mutual respect so long as the individuality of each remains important to you both. While you will have pride in each other's achievements, offer each to the other every help, encouragement, and support, you will remember that you have neither merged nor sub-merged your identities.

Thus, it is out of the balance between individuality and union, that love, whose incredible strength is equal only to its incredible fragility, is born.

Today's celebration of human affection is therefore the

outward sign of a sacred and inward commitment. It is a commitment that religious societies may consecrate and states may legalize, but which neither can create or annul. Such union can only be maintained by abiding will, and be renewed by human feelings and intentions. In this spirit these two persons stand before us.

The above ceremony doesn't really require elaboration. We come away from it with the feeling that Amy and David trust each other and trust their love for each other. The nature of their relationship is such that a statement of their feelings is the equivalent of a statement of commitment. The moment your feelings no longer lead logically to your commitment is the moment your relationship should be reexamined.

For two people to feel secure in a relationship that is premised on "commitment of intent," they must be without conflict about their love, and they must believe in their partner's love. Getting to the point where you would be comfortable with a marriage ceremony such as the one you just read can be hard work. The barriers to romantic love are plentiful and insidious. In Part II, I'll help prepare you for them.

PART II

The Barriers:

OPENING UP TO
ROMANTIC LOVE

CHAPTER 5

Fear of Romantic Loving—
Amoro-phobia

BEFORE YOU READ a word about amoro-phobia, look at the following quiz. On a sheet of paper number one through eighteen, and as you read each of the following statements write either "true" or "false" next to the appropriate number. Put the paper aside until you've finished reading Chapter 5. At the end of the chapter compare your answers with those I give in my discussion of the quiz.

Amoro-Phobia Quiz

1. I've never met the right man/woman, but I know exactly what he/she will look like.
2. All the really sexy men/women don't want to be in committed relationships.
3. As soon as you sleep with someone, things fall apart on a deeper level.
4. Powerful, masculine men/beautiful, sexy women just aren't very smart or sensitive.
5. All the good men/women are already taken.

6. There aren't any available men/women in (where you live).

7. I want to be taken care of and protected.

8. I'm not ready for a relationship.

9. Men/women don't find me attractive/interesting/etc.

10. I want someone who knows exactly how he/she feels about things and is consistent.

11. Change makes me nervous.

12. I'm looking for a hassle-free relationship.

13. If someone loves me, he/she won't care about how I look.

14. I need a lover who understands that my work comes first.

15. As soon as one thing goes wrong, everything falls apart.

16. All relationships get boring after the newness wears off.

17. There's no such thing as an enduring, intense romantic relationship.

18. As soon as someone knows you care, they take off.

What Is A Phobia?

We all know what it's like to be afraid of something. Fortunately our culture is reaching a point where even men are allowed to say that they're frightened without having an aspersion cast on their masculinity. We're coming to recognize that our fears frequently work to protect us. We talk about "a healthy fear of the water" when we admonish people not to swim out too far, or not to attempt a long swim when they're tired.

Still, there are such things as unhealthy fears: fears that paralyze us when we should be moving. Unhealthy fears—fears that are disproportionate to the events that trigger them—are called phobias. Extreme fears like these can severely limit our lives. When fears reach the point where they control you, rather than you controlling them, you really have no choice but to deal with them. Fortunately, psychologists are finding successful ways to help people deal with phobias. In the course of my work I've helped lots of people overcome unhealthy fears; and I've also come to recognize a common phobia that I've yet to read about in my professional journals—amoro-phobia.

Amoro-Phobia

Amoro-phobia is an extreme, unhealthy fear of romantic involvement. The fact is that all of us are frightened by the prospect of an intense romantic relationship; and some fear is usually warranted. Romantic love is risky. The kind of involvement I'm writing about requires a willingness to make yourself emotionally vulnerable to someone, and vulnerability is something we instinctively guard against.

We learn early in life that loving, which can give us the most intense pleasure, can also give us intense hurt. When we love someone we want things from them: contact, interaction, understanding, appreciation, availability, and affection. When we don't get what we want, and when we, ourselves, are ready to give of ourselves, it hurts. Since romantic love involves our deepest spiritual and sexual self, romantic rejection is frequently experienced as a profound rejection of the very heart of our identity. That sort of rejection is as painful as romantic love is pleasurable. The more we care, the more we risk.

Intense romantic love, then, involves enormous emotional risk. Amoro-phobics are people who become so obsessed with the possible pitfalls of romantic involvement that they forget about its potential for pleasure. Basically, there are two ways that amoro-phobia manifests itself: people can avoid romantic involvement entirely; or they can tune down the intensity of any involvement and assume that if they don't open themselves up to the extreme pleasure they'll be less vulnerable to extreme pain. They choose the easy and the safe.

Within each of these two categories of amoro-phobia are dozens of modus operandi: specific ways that amoro-phobics behave while they're trying to avoid romantic involvement. I call their behavior "disguises" because they're basically trying to cover up the fact that they're scared to death of intense romantic relationships. Frequently these disguises are so effective that the amoro-phobic isn't even aware of his fear. The idea of not being aware of your own fear is a little involved and requires an explanation.

I like to draw an analogy to Jackie Gleason's famous fear of flying. Despite the fact that Gleason's fear of flying is legendary, he has arranged his life in such a way that he never flies, never thinks about flying, and never even considers the possibility of flying. His phobia never causes him pain because he never allows himself to be in a situation in which he feels conflict. He needn't ever bother to think about "dealing" with his phobia.

In a similar way, severe amoro-phobics can manage never to confront their phobia. They may have established such an elaborate network of defenses to protect them from the pain that can come from romantic rejection that they are virtually never in a situation in which they might be subjected to the possibility of that pain. They avoid intense romantic relationships even before they present themselves.

Of course all of this subconscious avoidance—they don't know that they're avoiding love—doesn't really make their lives pain-free. If Jackie Gleason were bound and gagged and carried onto an airplane, he'd have to deal with his acrophobia. There is no similar situation through which an amoro-phobic might be forced to deal with his fear, but amoro-phobia has distinct fall-out results.

What might bring an amoro-phobic into a situation where he would seek help? Usually the people that come to see me feel depressed. They feel the non-specific, free-floating depression I discussed earlier. Others are driven into therapy by anxiety; again, it's free-floating. Some people somatize—they have all kinds of body aches and pains for which they can't find any explanation from their doctors.

Whatever it is that brings an amoro-phobic into therapy, it always takes an enormous amount of work before they are able to focus in on the problem—on the hole in their lives. Until an amoro-phobic reaches that point of recognition, all of the professional help in the world won't be of any value. I can't over-emphasize the degree to which these people suffer—the futility and hopelessness so many of them feel—before they understand the nature of their phobia.

Hopefully, in my discussion of "disguises" you'll be open either to recognizing some techniques that you use to avoid intense involvement or, at least, you'll recognize some techniques that people have used in their involvements with you. But before I get into specific ways amorophobics "protect" themselves from potential relationships, it's important to understand some of the origins of amorophobia.

Origins of Amoro-Phobia

Anyone who spends time with babies is moved by the intensity of their desires. When an infant cries for his mother his entire being trembles with neediness. When a three-year-old sees a toy she wants she'll spend the better part of the day asking for it: again and again and again. Young children, like puppies and kittens, are astoundingly tenacious about getting what they want, but their openness and high expectations leave them terribly vulnerable to disappointment. How often have you heard an adult say to a grieving child, "It's not the end of the world!"?

The first time a child hears the word "no" he's usually shocked. His confused face turns up as if to say, "You can't be serious." As the fact of denial sets in, the child's expression will run the gamut from surprise to confusion to insult and finally settle in on rage. "How dare you deprive me of something I want. It *is* the end of the world!"

Much of what we describe as the process of maturation involves learning to cope with postponed gratification and disappointment. We learn that we don't always get what we want when we want it; and sometimes we don't get what we want at all. This "education" can be a painful one, and some people get much more than their share of pain in growing up.

Virtually all of us respond to pain at some point by

withdrawing or retreating from what we perceive as its source. If someone kicks us in the face every time we approach him, it won't take long for us to stop approaching. We protect ourselves from hurt by lowering the intensity of our desires. After all, how hurt can you be about not getting something you don't care about having?

Margaret Mead and Margaret Bourke-White once did a study together in Bali. They were trying to uncover the root of stoicism that they considered common to the Balinese national character. They documented a common practice among mothers of young children on the island. These mothers would hold a "goodie" in front of their infants and withdraw it as soon as the baby began to reach for it. The first time they withdrew the "goodie" the infant would cry, but after they repeated the process many, many times the child became impassive. The procedure was finished when the baby stopped responding to the goodie entirely. The infants had learned, in this manner, to not want things intensely, because wanting only led to disappointment. By the time these children matured, the squelching of their personal desires had become totally ingrained.

Where does all of this tie in with romantic love? Amorophobias develop in much the same way as did the Balinese babies' lack of desire. People who were consistently disappointed in their earliest love attachments learned, during their childhood, that intense attachment only caused pain. Consider the case of James, a thirty-eight-year-old client of mine. James was extremely successful in the television industry and felt that, in most areas, his life was fulfilling. He began therapy because he was very much in love with a woman with whom he just couldn't manage to live. This was his third serious adult relationship and he couldn't help but notice an old pattern beginning to emerge. He would pick fights with the woman when they were together and essentially drive her away. Once she left him he missed her terribly and usually she'd return. She was deeply in love with James and had as hard a time being separated from him as he did being separated from her. Still, shortly after her return, the fighting would begin again.

It was an emotionally exhausting cycle, and he knew a time would come when she simply wouldn't return. In the course of therapy I learned that James had been deeply scarred when, at age eight, his father abandoned the family. The pain he felt when his father left was compounded by the suffering he witnessed in his mother. At that early age he vowed never again to care enough about someone to be hurt by his loss.

Thirty years later he experienced his intense relationship with a woman he loved as a terrible threat. The more he loved her, the more he struggled, unconsciously, to destroy the relationship. As he felt himself grow closer to this woman he instinctively picked a fight and managed to drive her away. He would pretend, both to himself and to his lover, that he didn't care about her, and it wasn't until after she broke things off and the "aloneness" set in that he recognized how much he valued the relationship.

Beginning with his father's abandonment he learned to "Balinese" himself. He took away what he loved and wanted and convinced himself that after a while he'd stop wanting it. Fortunately his need to love was strong enough, finally, to drive him to seek help. In therapy he confronted his problem, first by identifying it.

It's become almost a cliché today for people to end a relationship saying, "I love her but I can't live with her." Given that "love" is as precious as I think it is, it's enormously important to get beyond the cliché and ask "Why?" Why can't you live with someone you love? Why are you denying yourself that great pleasure? Does it involve your past experiences, a lack of reciprocity, or are you really not in love with this person?

Haunting Pasts

Observing the painful break-up of your parents' relationship doesn't necessarily result in amoro-phobia. Many youngsters learn to associate pain and romantic love from their own early experiences in relationships. Unhappy adolescent experiences can be traumatic. When you consider what a vulnerable time of life early adolescence is—with its physical growth and hormonal changes that leave us feeling like strangers in our own bodies—it's remarkable that we survive it at all; let alone use it as a time to reach out to another adolescent for self-confirmation. All the internal turmoil is compounded by the fact that adults rarely appreciate the extent of a teen-ager's suffering when their first tentative forays into romance don't work out.

The onset of intense sexual feeling that we experience in adolescence sets the stage for the development of our first feelings of romantic passion. All of our needs for companionship, friendship, the experience of our sexuality, the validation of ourselves in heterosexual relationships—all of our newborn hopes for romantic success and fulfillment— are focused on one person when, as an adolescent, we first fall in love. When we look back at those early relationships we may view them as "puppy love," but if those relationships resulted in a lowering of self-esteem, we may still bear their scars.

Consider the case of Thomas. At age thirteen Thomas was shy, easily embarrassed, likable, but very serious. While in the seventh grade he met a twelve-and-a-half-year-old girl named Jane, and was smitten with her. He found himself thinking about her constantly and running through the halls of his school to catch a glimpse of her.

One day he summoned up all of his courage and bravely wrote a note: "Dear Jane, I think you are beautiful and I love you. Thomas." He had stepped out of his protective shell and risked showing his feelings. He still remembers feeling helpless and exposed as he watched Jane read the note. She scribbled something on a piece of paper and passed it back to Thomas's desk. He unfolded the scrap of paper, his face flushed, and he read, "Dear Thomas, I think you are a jerk. Jane."

Today Thomas is forty-six years old and an extraordinarily guarded man. Although Jane wasn't the sole cause of his guardedness, his experience with her thirty-three years ago was enormously significant in his development. The energy of Thomas's adolescent passion was great enough to crack his shell of shyness and expose his inner feelings. Unfortunately, he was dealing with another adolescent who was both ill-equipped to deal with Thomas's emotions and insensitive to the courage it required for him to send the note. Thomas felt her response as a deep blow to his already shaky self-esteem.

Jane's insensitivity was only compounded by the way Thomas's parents dealt with this crisis in their son's life. His mother teased him for days about his "puppy love," and "wearing his heart on his sleeve." His father joined his mother, saying things like, "You're not going to let a *girl* get to you like that, are you?" What began as a heartfelt reaching out had been transformed into a demonstration of Thomas's weakness.

Amoro-Phobia and Men

This seems like a good time to discuss some romantic problems that are specific to men. It's as important for women, as it is for men, to understand the specific nature of men's phobias.

In many respects the problem of coping with romantic pain is much more difficult for boys than it is for girls. In our culture it is expected that women will value romantic attachments. It's also considered appropriate for women to cry and express sadness when they're disappointed or hurt. Boys, on the other hand, are taught to repress their emotions. As was the case with Thomas, they're often mocked for their romantic feelings. They're expected to be confident of their masculinity, rather than show such "unmasculine" feelings as confusion, doubt, or fear. Have you ever heard the expression "cocksure"?

Obviously, when someone is expected to be "too strong" to be hurt, it's a good idea to avoid situations where you might get hurt. Why take a chance with anything as important as your masculinity? Boys take chances because they're obligated to. The flip side of the coin that tells them not to show their emotions requires that they be the initiators of relationships. How safe can a teen-age boy be if he has to call up a girl and ask for a date? These very same boys who are not supposed to express their hurt have to initiate interactions in which they're very likely to get hurt. It's a rough situation.

Fortunately, many of the stereotypes that I grew up with are less rigid today. I hope the next generation of lovers won't have to contend with any of the problems with which we're frequently faced. But regardless of what the future has in store, *we* still have to get on with our relationships, and those old problems of expectations as defined by sexual roles are very much a part of our lives. Men today cannot just snap their fingers and slough off the unconscious messages of their childhood.

Not too long ago an extraordinarily successful, forty-year-old stockbroker named Adam came to see me. His second marriage was falling apart and he was disturbed by how little he felt. Basically he thought there might be something wrong with him because he had never really been in love. He and his first wife started having a hard time shortly after they were married and he spent much of their two years together sleeping with other women. His second marriage had a better beginning, but he lost interest in his wife after their son was born. Somehow, as soon as he "conquered" a women, he found himself unable to care very much.

I tried to get him to talk about his early romantic experiences and he consistently drew a blank. It wasn't until he'd been in therapy for several months that, in the middle of a session, he said, "Sondra Ellen Jimenko." Not "Sandy," not "What's-her-name," but "Sondra Ellen Jimenko," a full name and a remarkably full set of details to accompany this "dark lady."

Sondra was a girl Adam had gone steady with for a while when he was thirteen. He hadn't thought of her in years, but as soon as he started to talk about her he felt as though he couldn't stop. He described her appearance and experiences they had had together just as though he had seen her an hour before our session. Sondra had ultimately rejected Adam for a new boy in school and Adam was deeply hurt. When he talked about the experience with me he reexperienced his old hurt with an intensity he hadn't felt in years.

He recalled that his mother, just after he and Sondra broke up, had made fun of him in much the way Thomas's mother had. But Adam became particularly emotional when he remembered his father's reaction to his loss. His father went one step further than Thomas's did. He was horrified that a son of his could be so hurt by a girl and insisted that Adam go out and get himself two or three girlfriends immediately to demonstrate to the world how tough he really was. Basically Adam's father wanted his son to play the role of Lothario, a role he never succeeded at himself. Adam, who was invested in pleasing his father, followed his advice and put on a good show. He established quite a reputation as a "heart-breaker." In fact, what he actually did was repress his own pain, rather than acknowledge it, experience it, and resolve it.

For most of his adult life Adam continued to deal with women in much the way his father had advised. His repression of the experience with Sondra was so complete that he forgot the entire relationship until he recalled it again for me. Instead, he went through life rejecting women that he cared for, and busying himself with "lots" of other women. By the time he was twenty-seven he had blocked his feelings so effectively that he was convinced he had no feelings at all. His constant denial had saved him from deep hurt, at the cost of any good feelings he might have had. He came to therapy with a gnawing emptiness and the fear that he might go through his whole life without ever feeling anything.

I'm not suggesting by any means that men have cornered the market on amoro-phobia. Although men are clearly more vulnerable to some things that trigger amoro-phobia, there are lots of women with extreme and exaggerated fears of romantic involvement. The important thing to understand is that amoro-phobia grows from the pain we experience when we make ourselves vulnerable to another person. If we respond to romantic disappointment by withdrawing from love, then our fears will only grow.

Amoro-phobia Quiz Discussion

BY NOW YOU PROBABLY have some idea of how your fear of involvement expresses itself. Each of the questions in the quiz at the beginning of this chapter relates to one or more of the disguises we've just discussed. If you answered "true" to any of those eighteen statements you can begin to focus in on your problem. Let's look at each statement.

1. I've never met the right man/woman, but I know exactly what he/she will look like. If you agree with this statement, you're probably a "checklist" lover. Having a specific idea of what you want means two things: first, you're closing your eyes to lots of possibilities; and second, your list isn't coming from the center of your emotions—it's too intellectualized.

2. All the really sexy men/women don't want to be in committed relationships. On what basis does someone strike you as being sexy? If you're a "let's-keep-it-sexual" lover, it just may be that *you* only allow yourself to be attracted to people who aren't interested in committed relationships.

3. As soon as you sleep with someone, things fall apart on a deeper level. This statement is another indicator of the "let's-keep-it-sexual" lover. If you find that sex precedes the decline of most of your relationships, it's time to stop pointing fingers elsewhere and start looking toward yourself and your own attitudes. This statement might also signal a "thrill-of-the-hunt" lover. If you identify with this statement the most important thing you can do is begin asking yourself if you aren't the one who's losing interest after the sexual aspect of the relationship loses its newness.

4. Powerful, masculine men just aren't very sensitive. How do you define "masculine"? If you consistently find yourself involved with cruel men, and are *never* involved with men that you consider sensitive, it just may be that you're looking for a hard time. Why? Maybe because it precludes involvement.

5. *All the good men/women are already taken.* If you are in accord with this statement, you may be an "impossible partner" lover. The rationale is that since there are no appealing, *available* men/women you might as well look at the unavailable ones. The fact is that there are always available partners even though it may *feel* like there aren't. You have to differentiate between how you feel and reality.

6. *There aren't any available men/women in (where you live).* Unless you live in a tiny town and literally know everyone there, it's hard to make this kind of statement with any accuracy. Once again, you need to differentiate between your feeling and reality. It's possible that your fear of a relationship is tinting your view of the local population. If your statement is really accurate—if there really are no available, interesting men/women where you live—then why are you continuing to live there? If you're not in a relationship, but want to be, then it behooves you to live in an area where you're most likely to find one.

7. *I want to be taken care of and protected.* Once we become adults, we really have to take care of ourselves. Relationships that are predicated on "protection" have too many built-in problems. If you feel needy of care and protection you may express it by pushing too hard—as in the case of the "nice-to-meet-you-let's-get-married" lover—and drive people away.

8. *I'm not ready for a relationship.* How long have you been saying that? It may be a safe excuse for no involvement, and you may be an "I'm-not-good-enough" lover.

9. *Men/women don't find me attractive/interesting/etc.* There you are, "not good enough" again. If you think

you've got a great flaw in your character, either work it out or accept it and find someone else who will.

10. I want someone who knows exactly how he/she feels about things and is consistent. If you identify with this statement you should consider the possibility that you might be a "time cage," or "ivory tower" lover. No one, except for the most rigid of people, expects to be certain of everything, or locked into a set of feelings. People grow and change, unless they're too frightened to.

11. Change makes me nervous. Here again is a statement that might signal an "ivory tower" lover. Of course, change makes us all a bit nervous, but the issue is whether you attempt to stifle the change, or if you accept your nervousness and see where the change takes you.

12. I'm looking for a hassle-free relationship. No one is looking for a relationship that's riddled by problems, but if you honestly want a relationship that's problem-free, chances are you're a "never-care-too-much" lover. It's only when you don't really care, that problems don't present themselves.

13. If someone loves me he/she won't care about how I look. By now you recognize this statement as the signal of a "take-me-as-I-am" lover. The way you look is important, and it should be as important to you as it is to potential lovers. Statements like this one are part of an obstacle course that will keep you out of an intensely romantic relationship.

14. I need a lover who understands that my work comes first. Why set up a list of priorities, and, if you do, why expect anyone who loves you to accept second place with a smile? If you're a "work-aholic" lover, you may do such things to keep distance.

15. As soon as one thing goes wrong, everything falls apart. A "beat-your-partner-to-the-punch" lover is likely to believe this statement. Someone who's not terrified of everything disappearing is more likely to believe that "as soon as one thing goes wrong, you have to work at fixing it."

16. All relationships get boring after the newness wears off. This kind of statement is commonly heard among "thrill-of-the-hunt" lovers. New relationships are, indeed, exciting. But there's new-relationship excitement and old-relationship excitement, and it's important to learn about the latter. Otherwise, by definition, you'll never be able to find an enduring, exciting relationship.

17. There's no such thing as an enduring, intense romantic relationship. If you make this statement you probably have all sorts of arguments to back it up. Whatever your arsenal of proof may be, I know that you're wrong. If you've taken the trouble to construct your evidence into a good, cogent argument, you're probably leaning toward being a "love-is-trivial" lover.

18. As soon as someone knows you care, they take off. The logical conclusion of this statement, made most frequently by "never-care-too-much" lovers, is, "So don't let them know you care." That's a good formula for a lonely life. Consider the tragedy of two people who love each other spending their life together but never really expressing their loving feelings. It's easy to get caught in a cat-and-mouse game with regard to expressing feelings: if he/she tells me first, I'll tell him/her. That sort of contest most often ends with everyone feeling cheated.

CHAPTER 6

The Disguises of
Amoro-phobia

THERE ARE several important things to keep in mind when you read about the various disguises for amoro-phobia. Recognize that you adopted this behavior initially to protect yourself from romantic hurt. You chose the best way you could—either consciously or unconsciously—to take care of yourself. You need now to reevaluate how effectively your old mode of behavior is working for you today.

If you recognize yourself in the following pages (and virtually everyone will recognize herself to some degree), it probably means that your earlier attempts to protect yourself have started to work against you. By all means, please don't start beating your breast or obsessing about how hopelessly screwed-up you are. Don't concentrate on opportunities lost and accumulated guilt. That type of focus can actually become another way of avoiding romantic relationships. Lots of people are more comfortable living lonely, guilt-ridden existences than they are going out on a limb with another person.

Instead, try to utilize your new awareness. Consider how much your old defenses may be limiting your romantic life and how you want to move beyond those limitations. Try to pick up signal words or feelings in your romantic interactions that come just before you begin to withdraw, and consciously force yourself to fight them. Fighting a behavorial pattern that's become an ingrained aspect of your personality over an entire lifetime is, of course, enormously difficult. It requires, first and foremost, that you be painfully honest with yourself. It requires that you venture into unfamiliar territory alone, and risk having your feelings tampered with.

But that sort of "stepping out" is the only way you'll ever outgrow your problems. If you weren't feeling some dissatisfaction with your romantic life you wouldn't be reading this book, so the risks are worth something. You can always go back to your old behavior.

The Checklist Love—5'2" Eyes of Blue

Complete the following sentence: "The man/woman I love must be . . ." No doubt you have a ready response. To some extent all of us can come up with a "shopping list" to describe our ideal lover, and there's nothing wrong with having a good idea of the person with whom you envision yourself.

But lists can create problems, particularly if they originate more in your head than in your heart. When you operate from the head, rather than the heart, in a romantic relationship you may succeed in keeping your heart safe from hurt and keeping yourself safe from fear, but you sacrifice the potential of intense romantic love in the process. When you try to override your gut emotional response with what you think your emotional response *should* be, you're bound to end up in a problem relationship—if you have a relationship at all. Frequently lists become a way of avoiding real, personal involvement. Rather than dealing with your own internal needs, lists usually reflect cultural pressures. They frequently emphasize the *should*, and *shoulds* usually have to do with people other than yourself. Let's look at some problem lists:

List "A"

"I want a woman who's between 5'5" and 5'6" tall, with dark waist-length hair and a very tiny waist. I'd like her to have sort of dark, olive skin and to be very athletic and agile and smart. Also, I hate helpless women, so she needs to have a real career going. And last, but by no means least, she should *love* sex . . . but not have too much experience."

List "B"

"I'm not very fussy about what a man looks like but I do need a man who's very strong emotionally and always there for me. And it's crucial that he be successful in business, by which I mean he should earn more than $50,000 a year. He cannot be a work-aholic, he should be religious, and he'll have to live on the East Coast. Another thing that's important for me is that he be someone who wants to have children—at least four—and that he isn't much older than thirty-two."

The key to understanding the problems these lists create is to recognize the degree to which they *exclude*. Imagine that a friend of listmaker "A" approaches him with the prospect of a blind date. He describes the woman as vivacious, bright, attractive, and someone that he feels his friend would like. Listmaker "A" might say, "What color hair does she have?" "Let's see," his friend pauses for a moment to think. "She has kind of wavy short blond hair." End of conversation. End of possible relationship.

You can imagine a similar situation for listmaker "B"; let's add a twist. Suppose listmaker "B" is a designer who works with a young man, also a designer. The two of them sit side by side every day and have become very good friends. In addition to their growing friendship they are feeling more and more sexually drawn to each other. Finally, the man makes the move. They're out together for dinner and he says, "I think I've fallen in love with you."

Although she feels very much the same way she says, "I care for you very much as a friend but couldn't honestly say I'm in love with you." Why is she lying? Well, for one thing, he makes only $15,000 a year; and for another, he's the kind of man who acknowledges and talks about his fears and anxieties; hence, he doesn't *seem* strong emotionally. It's interesting to note that the very thing that makes this man attractive to listmaker "B" as a friend—his emotional openness—makes him unattractive as a lover.

Both of the above listmakers use their lists to stay out of intense romantic relationships. Listmaker "A" is so specific about his requirements that he, essentially, won't allow himself any involvement at all. Listmaker "B" has a more subtle problem. She does actually fall in love, but rejects her own feelings because they don't measure up to her list—a list that better reflects external pressures than internal voices. She's the type of amoro-phobic that may finally end up in a relationship with no intense romantic charge, but where all of the vital statistics measure up to her preordained standards. On a final tally sheet she's likely to be intellectually pleased, but emotionally empty.

Both listmakers need to reevaluate the purpose of their lists, as well as the purpose of their relationships. I've had dozens of clients come to me after they've fallen very much in love and say, "If you had asked me two years ago what kind of man/woman I wanted I'd have said a tall, thin, smooth-skinned artist. Here I am, head-over-heels in love with a short, stocky photographer who's hairy as a rug. And all I can think about is how great it feels when he hugs me, and how unappealing skin-and-bones-type men have become!"

If, in fact, you want to be in an intensely romantic relationship you have to keep yourself open. You don't have to tell yourself that you find someone attractive if your gut reaction is that you're turned off, but you have to be enough in touch with your gut-level reactions to really respond to them. You have to be able to separate your years of conditioning from your deeper reactions.

Opening yourself up to people really doesn't require any

great risk. If listmaker "A" went on the date his friend
proposed and found himself totally turned off to the woman
with short, wavy blond hair, no one would stand at his
back with a gun and force him to propose marriage. You
can always end a relationship that you feel is unfulfilling
. . . unless you were too frightened to begin it in the first
place.

The "Let's-Keep-It-Sexual" Lover

The "let's-keep-it-sexual" lover begins a relationship
by defining its limits. He or she (an ironic by-product of
the women's movement is that more and more women are
assuming this disguise) will divide the spiritual and physical aspects of an intense romantic relationship between two
different people and rigorously protect those divisions. A
woman who finds herself caring "too much" about her
"sexual lover" might interpret her caring as a signal to
end the relationship and look for someone else. Likewise,
if she suddenly finds herself to be physically attracted to a
man she calls "a very, very dear friend," she'll probably
start to create some emotional distance.

One traditional expression of the "let's-keep-it-sexual"
lover is what we call the "madonna-whore complex."
Men with this problem feel that women are either spiritual
(like a mother) or sexual (like a whore). Not only do these
men separate sex from emotional caring, but they label
sexual women as "bad." When a madonna-whore complex is covered by layers of unconscious denial, things can
become very complicated. Consider the confusion Tanya,
a woman I met at a workshop, felt:

"I had known Bob for nearly a year before we became
involved sexually. We were good friends. In fact, we
frequently talked about our problems with the opposite
sex. Our relationship became sexual when he was stuck in
my house one night during an electric storm. We'd both
had a bit much to drink and smoke and we suddenly found

ourselves in bed. And let me tell you . . . it was terrific. Just incredible.

"I woke up the next morning thinking 'This is too good to be true.' He woke up apologizing. When I suggested that he stop his apologizing and enjoy what we had he got really weird. For a while—a few days—he avoided me. Then, when he saw me, he said that he thought the sex would ruin our friendship. After protesting for a while we found ourselves—again—in bed. The sexual attraction was just too strong to repress.

"After a few encounters like that he did a turnabout. He accepted the sex, but really closed himself off emotionally. Finally he started treating me like shit. Really. He'd call me at midnight after spending the evening with another woman, and come over for a quick fuck, and not even spend the night. Now I just won't see him at all. I don't have to put up with that.

"The sad thing is that it seems like he was right. The sex did ruin the relationship. But I still don't see why it had to."

The sex had to ruin the relationship for Bob because he's terrified of a full romantic relationship. He won't lower his guard enough to care for, and be cared for by one woman. By spreading his neediness among several women he feels less vulnerable.

As I said earlier, I don't base my objection to lust relationships on any moral ground. Usually, however, after a string of relationships limited exclusively to sex, people end up feeling profoundly empty. A life-style of one-night stands (or two-week or two-month stands) is one thing when you're twenty and quite another when you're forty.

Assuming that you find willing partners who satisfy you sexually, sexual satisfaction without emotional involvement simply can't last long. Much of the excitement in these relationships is connected with conquest and novelty, neither of which stimuli can endure. In a truly intense romantic relationship, however, the sexual drive is literally nourished by an emotional involvement.

"Give Me Some Men Who Are Cruel, Heartless Men"

There are people who always manage to get involved with cruel or abusive partners. I'm not talking here about masochists. Clinically, masochists want to be involved with people who hurt them; they "get off on" their suffering. I've seen lots of men and women in my practice who seem to always be mistreated in their love relationships, and who take absolutely no pleasure in their mistreatment.

"How do they always seem to find me?" a woman asked, her face stained with tears, after she described her last romantic involvement to her therapy group. She had been involved, for a year, with a man who consistently mocked her stupidity/inadequacy/incompetence, etc.

After a great deal of discussion it was clear that she maintained an involvement with her cruel lover because his cruelty kept her own involvement down to a certain level. Because she would never make herself truly vulnerable to a cruel man, her involvement with such men kept her "safe" from intense romantic love.

Amoro-phobics will frequently get involved in relationships that have built-in limits. I've seen an instance in which a true phobic got involved with a cruel partner who actually began to change and become softer. The phobic ended the relationship claiming, "I didn't trust the change that came over him." In fact, what she doesn't trust is her own ability to be in an intense relationship. She actually went out and found a new lover who treated her as cruelly as the previous one had.

The "Impossible-Partner" Lover

One sure way of never having to risk rejection is to only involve yourself with relationships that can't become intense romantic relationships. If, for example, you consistently fall in love with married people, you're essentially safe from further involvement. As long as your lover remains married, you needn't be concerned with the demands of a consuming, no-holds-barred involvement. There's always a certain distance that brings with it a sense of safety.

Another aspect of the "impossible-partner" lover is the man or woman who doesn't get involved in an intensely romantic relationship until after they're married. The same principle applies in this case. The safety of a marriage that isn't intense makes it possible to be involved in a more intense relationship.

It's no surprise that these relationships frequently fall apart if the married person gets divorced. As soon as an intense romantic relationship becomes viable all sorts of blemishes become apparent. Of course, marriage isn't the only circumstance that might make someone attractive to an "impossible-partner" lover. An amoro-phobic of this variety may fall in love with someone who lives halfway around the world. Another might fall in love with inaccessible movie stars, powerful political figures, or homosexuals. There are even some people who send proposals of marriage to criminals on Death Row.

The issue of the "impossible-partner" lover is always one of tangible inaccessibility. If you were to ask him/her why he/she wasn't in a viable romantic relationship the answer would be something like: "I'm ready. But I only meet married men." If you counter with, "Why get involved with married men in the first place?" they might retort with "*All* the good ones are married." It's a full-cycle, no-win situation that spells out a-m-o-r-o-p-h-o-b-i-a.

The "Nice-To-Meet-You-Let's-Get-Married" Lover

How can I possibly call someone who proposes on the first (second? third?) date an amoro-phobic? It's easy. First of all marriage need not have anything to do with intense romantic love—unfortunately. And second, anyone who proposes to a stranger—assuming the stranger is sane—should expect a firm negative response. I'd go so far as to say that anyone who proposes to a stranger can probably expect that his/her phone number will have been changed when next you call!

There is the rare exception which involves the phenomenon of love at first sight. I discussed that almost magical occurrence at length in Chapter 1. A person can look at a stranger, feel an extraordinary attraction and *know*—just as sure as she knows her own feelings—that the object of her excitement has the potential of feeling the same thing. This phenomenon is very different from what happens with the "nice-to-meet-you-let's-get-married" lover.

The purpose of the "nice-to-meet-you-let's-get-married" lover is precisely to frighten people away. There's a neediness in his/her proposal that somehow says, "Nothing you ever do for me will be enough." The trick this phobic plays on himself is that when he/she is rejected he/she can say, "I was willing to make myself vulnerable but it's impossible to find anyone else who wants a committed relationship these days."

The "Super-Hostile" Lover

First cousin to the "nice-to-meet-you-let's-get-married" lover is, oddly enough, the "super-hostile" lover. In each case the idea is to create a situation in which you'll be rejected; a situation that will help you avoid an intense romantic relationship. This type of amoro-phobic never actually does the rejecting himself. He never says, "I want to stop seeing you." Rather, he gets the other person to do his dirty work so that he (or she) can avoid the burdensome feelings of guilt or responsibility.

Consider the following situation. Nancy and Eric are out with another couple. During the course of the evening, Eric finds every opportunity to put Nancy down in front of her friends. If they talk about cooking, Eric jokes about how bad Nancy's cooking is. If they talk about music Eric will have everyone in stitches with a story of Nancy's inability to carry a tune. When they talk about sex, Eric makes fun of Nancy's lack of sexual experience and her shyness.

When they get home that night Nancy explodes. "I just won't take any more of this. I can't stand being the brunt of all your jokes. I won't take it anymore. I want to separate." Eric is shocked. "What are you talking about?" he asks. "You know I care about you more than anyone else. I was just being social." "Bullshit," Nancy says (at least, we'd hope that's what Nancy would say).

Poor Eric. Nancy didn't take the trouble to understand him. Or, better yet, Poor Eric. Nancy had no sense of humor. Or even, Poor Eric. Why do women have to be so super-sensitive?

In fact, Eric got precisely what he should have expected, and precisely what he probably wanted. He got out of an involvement. He can feel sorry for himself if he chooses. And he can feel angry at Nancy for rejecting him. Finally, he can feel like it's not really his fault at all. The only problem with all of those feelings is that they don't give him the warmth that a loving relationship does.

The "I'm-Not-Good-Enough-For-You" Lover

There are some amoro-phobics who are very good at rejecting. The key to their rejecting is that they do it for the "good of" the other person. At least *they say* they're doing it for the good of the other person. When this sort of amoro-phobic says, "I'd like to be in a relationship with you but I'm just too fucked-up now. You really deserve more than I can give you," I usually can't help but agree.

She's right. She *is* too disturbed to be in a relationship now. The question is, "When will you *not* be too disturbed to be in a relationship?" I've known people who managed to elude relationships by bemoaning their own inadequacy for years and years. The thing that makes these people qualify as true amoro-phobics—and the thing that makes their honest plea into a fairly shallow disguise—is that they never really attempt to do anything about their problem. Rather, they hold on to it and use it again, and again, and again.

These people use their own feelings of worthlessness to keep others away. If they meet someone who says, "I'd like to stay with you while you work out your problems," they run scared. "No," they might say. "I've really got to do this alone." Then they get involved in another relationship which goes to the same point of involvement and ends because, "I'm too fucked-up for you."

"Time-Cage" Lovers

"Time-cage" lovers don't allow relationships to grow and change, for fear of losing them. The fact is that a fear of letting your relationship grow and change is a fear of real intense romantic relationships. Growth and change are integral parts of such relationships, and trusting the direction of your partner's growth should be at the root of your love.

The problem of time-cage lovers frequently shows itself among couples that married very young and have been involved in a relationship of decreasing intensity for many years. A phrase that signals the time-cage phobia is, "She's not the same girl she was twenty years ago," or "He's a different guy than the one I fell in love with." Unfortunately, many people who find themselves faced with this problem get divorced and proceed to look for relationships that are guaranteed to not change with time.

Simply put, there is no such relationship. People change with time. You can't fight it and shouldn't even want to. The key to overcoming this phobia is in accepting the fact of growth and change and thereby being more sensitive to it. No one changes overnight. We change slowly, bit by bit. We evolve. If you're aware of, and sensitive to the person you love you'll be able to talk about changes as they happen and adjust to them. You may even be excited by the way your lover is growing. The only way you can wake up next to a stranger one day, after living with that person for a long time, is if your eyes have been closed.

The "Ivory-Tower" Lover

"Ivory-tower" lovers have a great deal in common with "time-cage" lovers. They're both obsessed with a fear of change. An "ivory-tower" lover wants to go, with his love, to a safe place where the world with all its intrusions won't threaten his relationship.

Just as there is no way of escaping time, however, there's no way of escaping the problems that life imposes. Relationships should be pliable enough to accommodate different environments. If a relationship works well in one city, there's no reason to assume that it will all fall apart because you have to move to another city.

"Ivory-tower" lovers are frequently jealous. I'll deal with jealousy in greater depth later, but suffice it to say that a relationship is not a genuinely intense romantic relationship if the presence of other men or women is considered a threat. We're surrounded by other people. Our lives are richer because of our relationships with them. As soon as we feel like isolating ourselves from the people around us (and taking our lover hostage in this isolation), then our relationship is in trouble.

"Never-Care-Too-Much" Lovers

How many times have you gone into a relationship with the idea that you wouldn't let yourself care much anyway. "I just want to have a good time." "I'm looking for an *easy* relationship." "I want a relationship where there aren't a lot of demands on me."

Of course, there's nothing wrong with wanting to have a good time in a relationship. I'm the first one to say that "good times" are what love relationships are all about. The problem comes when having a good time is equated with "not caring too much." "Never-care-too-much" lovers are assuming that if they don't care, they won't get hurt. There are lots of problems with that assumption.

First of all, "caring" is not an intellectual process. You can't say to yourself, "I don't care," when your feelings are saying, "I do care." If someone that you claim to not care about ends a relationship, you're going to be in pain, no matter how much you tell yourself that he/she didn't mean much to you.

Second, if you do succeed in finding a relationship that you don't care about, and if that is the extent of your relationship, then you suffer an even greater loss. You suffer a life without a really loving relationship. You suffer having to spend all of your time with someone that doesn't really matter very much to you. Your feelings, after a while, will be beyond safe. They'll be eradicated.

Caring is at the heart of any relationship, whether it be romantic or platonic. Teaching yourself not to care is like teaching yourself not to eat after a particularly bad case of food poisoning. We can't deprive ourselves of the nourishment that comes with good food or good relationships, without feeling the ill effects.

"Take-Me-As-I-Am" Lover

Not too long ago a woman attending one of my workshops stood up to talk about why she had trouble finding relationships. She said that she could not find men who were willing to accept her "for what I am." She went on to say that she would never feel secure about a relationship if she believed it was predicated on some major alteration of her inner self.

Sounds reasonable, doesn't it? There's just one problem. This woman was grossly overweight. She was thirty-one years old and had been obese for the last fifteen years. She had turned her fat into a "fidelity test." True love meant loving every pound. Only once her knight in shining armor passed the test of loving her poundage would he qualify for her coveted hand.

An interesting aside on this woman is that when I asked her to name the men in the room whom she found attractive she named the three most conventionally attractive, slender men in the group.

The question I pose to "take-me-as-I-am" lovers—whether their issue is weight, personal hygiene, or sour personalities—is, "Why do you need to set up a test?" If I told you that I had a first date with a woman and prepared for it by chewing a couple of cloves of raw garlic and rubbing my body with whale oil, "Just to make sure she was interested in the real me," you'd think I was either somewhat screwy or very invested in making my first date my last. And, of course, you'd be right.

People who are not afraid of relationships look for ways to make the formation of those relationships easier; they don't design obstacle paths for potential lovers. If you smell bad and are about to meet someone who interests you, you take a shower. If you're obese and you really want to meet potential lovers, you *make an effort* to make yourself more attractive. To most of the world, being overweight makes you less attractive.

The "Work-aholic" Lover or "I-Gave-At-The-Office" Lover

Most work-aholics (which I differentiate from "hard workers") don't have room in their lives for an intense romantic relationship. They've already allocated their most intense energies to their work. They choose to get their emotional fulfillment in the office.

I consider a fulfilling career to be an enormously important factor in a well-rounded, healthy life. But there's no question that work can easily become the convenient excuse for amoro-phobics to avoid relationships. A thirty-six-year-old corporate lawyer who was a partner in a prestigious New York law firm once described his average workday as beginning at nine A.M. and ending between 11:30 and midnight. He went on to say that he worked at least six days a week. He insisted that this schedule was absolutely necessary to his success, and that ever since his divorce he'd had a hard time meeting women.

He recently called me to say that he was remarrying. "Terrific!" I said. "I'm delighted for you." "Yes," he said in a businesslike voice. "She's very attractive and we seem to get along rather well. She gets on with my family and I get along with hers. We seem to be able to resolve our problems in an amicable way and she's familiar with my life-style because her ex-husband was a corporate lawyer. All in all we seem to be compatible and the relationship doesn't make any demands on my work schedule."

"Are you in love?" I asked. "I think we'll have a reasonably happy life together," he answered. "But are you in love with this woman?" I asked again. "We're very compatible," he repeated, and since he wasn't a client, I didn't push the issue.

The "Beat-Your-Partner-To-The-Punch" Lover

There's nothing that frightens the "beat-your-partner-to-the-punch" lover as much as the idea of being rejected. This variety of phobic is so finely tuned to his lover's dissatisfaction that he/she occasionally picks it up even before it exists. The modus operandi involved here is: reject him before he rejects you.

I have a client who typifies this problem. She's been involved with a man for the last six months and was just beginning to really let herself relax with him. She hadn't felt as much for a man in many years, and her vulnerability terrified her. At one point she came into the session and said, rather bluntly, "I'm going to break up with Tony." I was surprised. Things had been going so well just a week earlier and I asked her to explain.

She began, "I just feel that we reached some kind of peak and he's beginning to lose interest. I notice him looking at other women. He seems less passionate in our lovemaking. And I'm just not clear that he's the kind of man I want to spend my life with."

"Well, which is it?" I pushed a bit. "Have you lost interest in him or has he lost interest in you? And who's talking about your whole life? I didn't know you'd reached that point yet!"

"Well," she said quickly, "we're getting very close."

"And you're scared to death," I concluded.

She nodded. After a few moments she added, considerably less coolly than she had begun, "I'd rather be the one to end it now, than take the chance that he'll end it in a month or so."

When I asked for more evidence that he was dissatisfied with the relationship she couldn't really give any. Still she was ready to discard the relationship rather than risk rejection. On some level the "beat-your-partner-to-the-punch" lover doesn't feel entitled to the kind of happiness that comes with an intense romantic relationship. She can't experience the pleasure without feeling unworthy of it; and that "unworthy" feeling translates into the feeling that the relationship isn't going to last.

The final step of this unconscious circle of thought is, "As long as it's going to end, why should I sit around and wait for it to happen? I might as well take the bull by the horns and end it myself." People who are certain that disaster is going to come frequently create the disaster themselves. We call this a self-fulfilling prophecy.

Still, a "beat-your-partner-to-the-punch" lover has to face the possibility that her suspicions may be right. What if her lover is thinking of ending the relationship? The fact remains that you can survive rejection— as painful as that is—a lot better than you can survive never gambling on a relationship. If it's an intense romantic relationship you're after, you're more likely to find one if you wait and see what happens, than if you cut off all potential relationships prematurely.

The "Thrill-Of-The-Hunt" Lover

A "thrill-of-the-hunt" lover illustrates Groucho Marx's dictum: "I wouldn't want to be a member of any club that would have me as a member." This particular phobic finds himself enormously attracted by what he/she can't have: forbidden fruit, the unknown, the exotic. As soon as they have what they're after it's no longer unattainable and they lost interest.

The root of this problem is low self-esteem. Such a man, for example, is always trying to prove himself sexually by "scoring" with women who will—just by accepting him—give testimony to his sexual prowess. The problem is that we can't give each other self-esteem. We can only give that, in a significant way, to ourselves.

After a man with low self-esteem has conquered his "number 10," his old feelings of inadequacy will, inevitably, return. At that point he'll start picking "number 10" apart. "She may be beautiful," he'll say to himself, "but she's stupid. No wonder I was able to snare her. I need a woman who's both good looking and very intelligent."

Good-bye "number 10." When he deals with his low self-image, he'll no longer look for women to verify it; nor will he blame them for his inadequacy. The modus operandi of conquer and reject leaves little opportunity for intense romantic involvement. You can't form significant human attachments when you're busy scoring points. Until you can appreciate the value of intimacy, which comes hand-in-hand with self-esteem, you'll never get beyond the thrill of newness.

The Intellectual "Love Is Trivial" Phobic

Don't confuse people who use their intellects as a defense against romantic love with true intellectuals. Amoro-phobics of this variety may, or may not be intellectuals. And conversely, intellectuals may, or may not be amoro-phobics. This amoro-phobic builds elaborate, rational arguments denying the possibility of such a thing as intense romantic love.

Most of the arguments conclude that the sort of love I'm talking about is frivolous, trivial, or silly. The question you must stop and ask, if you hear yourself railing against the existence of no-holds-barred, head-over-heels, passionate romantic love is, "Why am I bothering to construct this anti-love argument? What's the motivation behind my ardent protest?''

Most such arguments stem from a very strong cultural bias against selfishness. "With all the pain and suffering and deprivation in the world today," this bias goes, "can't you think of a more productive way to spend your energies than in pursuit of the perfect relationship and your own personal happiness?"

The "love-is-trivial" phobic doesn't understand that intense, enduring romantic love is, and should be entirely selfish in nature, and that this sort of love doesn't require any justification whatsoever. You don't need to prove that you might be more valuable to society if you were in an intense romantic relationship (although I happen to believe this). The issue of your contribution to society and the issue of what you get from a love relationship are entirely separate.

It may be of some interest to point out that the "pursuit of happiness" is a right that is guaranteed in our Declaration of Independence. This pursuit was a radical idea when the Declaration of Independence was drafted, and it remains a radical idea today. I am of the firm belief that there is nothing more noble than attempting to secure happiness for yourself in a love relationship with another person. Rather than feel the need to justify that healthy, selfish pursuit, you should feel proud that you have the courage to attempt it.

CHAPTER 7

Minimizing Amoro-phobia

YOU ARE an amoro-phobic. Welcome to the club. It's not, I'm afraid, a very exclusive club. As I've said before, virtually all of us have been members. In the last chapter I discussed the most common disguises for amoro-phobia. You may have an entire wardrobe of those disguises in your closet. They're classic mix-and-match coordinates. Sometimes it's hard to discern where one picks up and another leaves off. Sometimes it's hard to even know you're wearing one. They can fit like a second skin. In fact, the ones you've been wearing longest may even have quietly crept *under* your skin.

Your primary task is to learn to recognize your own personalized wardrobe of disguises. Until you recognize them, label them clearly, and are able to feel the moment you assume them, they'll continue to rule your life. Unfortunately the entire process of disguising your fears is often unconscious. Unpeeling defenses you've spent years developing can be a difficult job, but *it is a job you can do successfully*. There is absolutely no question that if you do your emotional homework and commit yourself to the long-term task of turning your amoro-phobia around, you will be able to find a place in your life for enduring, intense romantic love. You can change.

Take It Easy On Yourself/Push Yourself Harder

Once you've determined intellectually to change your loving ways, you'll have to find a proper balance in your effort to deal with your phobia. Remember, you became an amoro-phobic in an effort to take care of yourself: to protect yourself. You didn't become an amoro-phobic because you wanted to hurt other people or be emotionally deprived. If you are intent on finding romantic fulfillment, you'll have to accept yourself as you are and avoid getting caught in a trap of self-blame. If your inclination is to be very hard on yourself, you'll have to keep in mind that healing requires thought and kindness. The "I'm-not-good-enough-for-you" lover spends his life feeling guilty while he attempts to get his act together, and it's not unlikely that his guilt is the major factor interfering with the resolution of his problems. Letting go of guilt and self-blame will free-up an enormous amount of energy.

I'm stressing the issue of guilt and self-blame because I know that focusing on guilt creates major problems in dealing with a phobia—whether it's a fear of water, flying, or romantic involvement. With phobias other than amoro-phobia this sort of unhealthy focus is usually less subtle and easier to deal with. Someone will come to me and say, "I know this is stupid of me, but I'm terrified of airplanes." I can address the issue immediately by saying, "Fear has nothing to do with intelligence or stupidity. Let's talk about the fear, not your I.Q."

Amoro-phobia, however, is usually much more subtle and complex than other phobias. For one thing an amoro-phobic, with his/her wardrobe of disguises, is less likely to be aware of the source of fear than other phobics. We tend to feel more ashamed of our lack of romantic involvement and frequently think of ourselves as inadequate human beings. Those feelings of shame make it very important to create elaborate defenses and to deny our fear. It seems that just when we should be gentle with ourselves—just as we are attempting to make ourselves more vulnerable than we've been in a long, long time—is when we come down hardest on ourselves.

The other side of this coin is the kind of amoro-phobic who doesn't accept any responsibility for his/her problem, who may, in fact, blame others, and who is much too easy on himself. Whichever category you fall into, it's crucial to find the proper balance. One of the techniques I use to minimize amoro-phobia involves writing messages to yourself on a 3 x 5 index card and tucking it into a pocket or purse. Message number one is: TAKE IT EASY ON MYSELF. THIS IS HARD WORK. Or, PUSH MYSELF A LITTLE BIT MORE, EVEN THOUGH IT'S HARD TO DO.

Set Reasonable Goals

"Taking it easy on yourself" means, first of all, recognizing that in order to overcome your amoro-phobia you must allow yourself to progress both purposefully, and slowly. Even if there remains some minimal remnant of your fear, you can be cured functionally. You can open up your life to intense, enduring romantic love.

One important aspect in dealing with your fear involves an appreciation of the progress you're making and an understanding of the healing process. This means that you must learn to allow for setbacks. Any gain is real, and shouldn't be discounted by the fact that you may have had a setback. If you continue to plow away at your problems, the setbacks will diminish in both intensity and in duration.

The first step in learning to control your phobia, rather than have it control you, is to set some viable goals, keeping in mind that your ultimate goal is to be in control of your fear. The kinds of goals you set are important. At this point, it's a good idea to liken yourself to an athlete who's beginning training. A marathon runner, for example, doesn't wake up on day one of training and run twenty-six miles. He builds up to his goal slowly, with small increments each day. If he undertakes too much at one time, he may pay for it with a sprain or a bad knee. He may actually miss a race because he pushed himself too hard.

Phobias are most effectively dealt with in similar increments. You have to build up slowly to the point where you
feel comfortable opening up to someone emotionally and
sexually.

I once had a client who typified the "let's-keep-it-sexual"
lover. Aaron was thirty-four when he first came to see me
and he had never been in a long-term relationship of any
sort. He tired of women after a few months and as soon as
his eye caught an attractive new prospect he would leave
his old lover and begin a new pursuit. He began therapy
because he was lonely. Most of his friends were married,
or getting married, a few had children, and he felt that he
had spent so much time running around the same track that
his footsteps had created a rut.

Once we got to a point where he identified himself as a
"let's-keep-it-sexual" lover he became determined to change
his way. His method, unfortunately, was rather extreme.
He decided that he wouldn't have sexual relations with a
woman until he'd been dating her for several months.
"That way," he reasoned, "my interest will build up and
I will be able to guard against my old pattern."

Despite my objections to Aaron's plan he pursued it and
found he was getting involved only with women he found
*un*attractive sexually. He developed good, caring friendships, but when the time came for sex he wasn't interested. He didn't really deal with the issue of meshing his
sexual and emotional needs. Every now and then when he
met a woman that really turned him on he'd go out with
her once and then drop her. His way of dealing with his
phobia simply created new problems. It didn't bring him
any closer than he had been to finding an intense romantic
relationship.

A different game plan for Aaron—one that might have
worked—would have been to continue to date women that
he found attractive and, assuming that they were interested
in him, to pursue his sexual relationships *along with* emotional relationships. Aaron wasn't really dealing with anything in his decision to date women he didn't find attractive.
He was still restricting himself to one-dimensional rela-

tionships. The issue he had to face was one of integrating two aspects of a relationship, not trading in one kind of isolation for another.

I Can Do It, I Can Do It, I Can Do It

I've emphasized throughout this book the importance of using your head when you pursue an intense romantic relationship. Using your head means that you must learn to be aware of gut, emotional reactions you have that keep you out of relationships. Once you're aware of these reactions you have to continue to use your head to change them.

There's a classic children's book that illustrates my point. The book, by Watty Piper, is called *The Little Engine That Could,* and it's about an engine pulling a trainload of toys over a mountain to a village with lots of children. The engine breaks down and the toys implore several passing engines to pull them over the mountain. Each engine they stop has a reason for not being able to help: one only pulls passenger cars; one only pulls freight; a third is too old and tired. Finally, a tiny blue engine chugs alone. Nobody thinks the little engine will be able to pull the train all the way up the mountain, but the engine is eager to try.

"She thought of the good little boys and girls on the other side of the mountain who would not have any toys or good food unless she helped. Then she said, 'I think I can, I think I can, I think I can, I think I can.'

"Finally, after a great effort and lots of old-fashioned positive thinking, the engine made it over the mountain and down to the village with her cargo.

"And the Little Blue Engine smiled and seemed to say as she puffed steadily down the mountain, 'I thought I could, I thought I could, I thought I could, I thought I could, I thought I could, I thought I could.' "

*   *   *

Essentially, we've got to get our engines in gear and start *consciously* pushing ourselves to do things. A children's book may seem a bit simplistic, but the essence of overcoming amoro-phobia is very simple. Understanding what you have to do isn't difficult. Doing it, is another story. And there's no better way to tackle your problems than to begin telling yourself that you can do it, you can do it, you can do it.

Using Your Fear

Something incredibly, wonderfully terrifying has happened. You finally agreed to meet a man your sister's brother-in-law used to work with. You hate blind dates and managed to put this one off for almost a year, but you ran out of excuses. When your sister said, "What have you got to lose?," you simply couldn't think of a thing. So you went.

And you had the best time you can remember having with a man. Conversation never lagged. You found him enormously attractive. You also know that he's very excited about you. This could very well be the man you've been waiting for. But there's a problem. The entire situation is scaring you to death.

How do you know that you're frightened? You're much too well-protected to be trembling in your shoes. It's no simple matter, detecting your fear. But you've made a recent study of yourself and are getting very adept at picking up even your most subtle signals. You know that you tend to be a "super-hostile" lover and by the end of your first evening with "Mr. Right" you were beginning to put him down. He's a bit on the short side of 5'7", and when he said casually that he had been somewhat of a jock in college, you asked—with a snide little grin—if he was captain of the basketball team.

Fortunately, the moment the words slipped past your lips you heard them for what they were. They weren't a joke. There's nothing a mature adult could possibly find

humorous in teasing another mature adult about height. They
were, rather, a warning siren of your fear pattern. They
were your own subconscious grabbing you by the shoulders, shaking you, and saying, "What the hell are you
doing? You like this guy. Why are you beginning to push
him away?"

Perhaps your fear signal is something other than hostility. The issue is not specific to any one signal. Rather, it's
that you learn what happens to you when you're frightened
by a potential romantic relationship, and that you counter-
act your old knee-jerk response by one that is more thought
out. I can help you learn a new response, but until you
recognize and meet the old one with "I think I can, I think
I can, I think I can," none of my techniques will work.
You have to think and to understand that you can overcome your fear before you actually succeed in doing so.

It's In The Cards

As I mentioned earlier, one of the techniques I use to
minimize amoro-phobia involves writing messages to yourself on 3 x 5 index cards and carrying the cards around
with you. However corny or contrived this technique may
sound to you at first, my experience indicates that it does
work. We need all the help we can get when we attempt to
overcome an ingrained fear, and these cards can frequently
be the pat on the back, the reassuring nod, or simply the
reminder that we very much need in the heat of battle. In a
therapy session people frequently understand something in
a new way. The real success of therapy entails learning to
focus on these new understandings when you need them in
life. A card can help deliver that and speed up the activity
of therapy significantly. It's easy to be clear and logical
about our problems when we're sitting in our safe, comfortable living rooms. It's less easy when our husband is
sitting there with us; when we're about to go out with
someone we care about; when we feel our hearts pounding
in our heads and our every impulse is to turn around and
run.

At no point should you have a pocket sagging under the weight of fifty index cards. Nor should you have to shuffle through a stack looking for the appropriate message. That's *not* the way these cards are meant to be used. Rather, each card should be written, carried with you, and filed away. If you have a setback, you'll be able to reuse cards. It's unreasonable to expect to overcome a time-honored behavior problem in one day. You'll have to drill on each card until you eradicate your old responses, and that can be awhile.

The act of writing a positive message to yourself can be as important as looking at that message eight hours, eight days, or eight months later. If you believe what you're writing—great. If you don't, you'll be surprised by how much you internalize while you're jotting a message down.

How do you know which card to bring with you when? Essentially, the use of these cards requires good, common sense. If, for example, you have a date with someone you've never met before and you know that your inclination is to make quick judgments in such situations, you might pack a card that says: DON'T JUDGE. STAY OPEN. Such a card doesn't guarantee that you won't judge; but it does mean that you're less likely to be unconscious to the fact that you *are* judging. It will heighten your awareness.

In order to use these cards effectively you must learn to anticipate. If you have a fight with your husband when he comes home from work late, write a note to yourself at six o'clock (or when he calls to say he'll be late) saying: COOL IT. A TEN-HOUR WORKDAY IS HARD ON US BOTH. Make sure the note is in your pocket when you greet him. It will help!

In my practice I design the content of a client's cards precisely in order to meet his or her needs, and I help teach my clients to design their own cards. You will learn, as they do, to write and tailor cards for yourself. In addition to very personalized cards, there are those which, in a very general way, deal with the nature of a phobia. These supportive cards are part of the *basic pack*. They apply to nearly every amoro-phobic.

The Basic Pack

Pay attention to my fear. No one knows what's going on inside you better than you. What are your fear signals? Do you become hostile? Do your palms sweat? Do you feel faint? Do you take on an amoro-phobic disguise? Learn to recognize your signals so that you can open up to a new response. Make your fear work *for* you.

Beware of behavior that takes me away from my fear. The point of recognizing your fear is *not* so you can obliterate it. Any of your old phobic responses can make you feel less frightened; and those are the responses you want to stay away from. Believe it or not, what you need to do is feel *more* frightened. You're scared because something good is happening.

Courage means facing fears. There it is again. It's good to be scared. It means that something new is happening, that you've opened yourself up a bit more than you ever have before.

Make myself uncomfortable. Making yourself uncomfortable is another way of giving yourself a little push. Remember, I'm not an advocate of pushing too hard. But if you're too comfortable it probably means you're wearing a pair of old shoes instead of breaking in new ones. You need to edge out on a limb, inch by inch, and to feel a bit uncomfortable.

Look for people whose rejection would hurt me. There's an old joke: go out with an ugly man/woman. It won't feel as bad when he/she leaves you. The joke represents a safe but uneventful life-style. If the loss of your lover won't hurt you, then you're not involved with the right lover. If you care, then the loss will hurt. If you don't care, it's not worth your time.

* * *

Say things I've never said. Saying things that you've always been too uncomfortable to say is a good indicator of romantic involvement. One thing you might say when you're feeling scared is, "I'm feeling scared." The important thing is to be honest and just ever-so-slightly uncomfortable.

Being hurt won't kill me. This is, perhaps, the most important card. You often feel like a romantic blow will actually be the end of you. It won't. You need to be quite literal on this matter. You will not die if someone you love doesn't love you back. You'll hurt, to be sure, but you'll also recover from your hurt. The point of this card isn't to diminish the pain of romantic rejection. Rather, it's to keep it in some sort of perspective. That perspective is crucial if you are to go on with your life.

I can tolerate more pain than I think. This is the card to keep handy if you're in the process of a difficult break-up. It's a reminder of your strength. When you're feeling vulnerable you tend to underestimate your strength. "If John won't see me tonight I think I'll have a breakdown." In fact, we all have hidden stores of strength to draw upon when we need them. We *do* survive.

Knowing that I'll survive hurt makes me even stronger. This card is like a booster shot. It amplifies the reward of all your risk-taking. It feels good to approach relationships from a position of strength, and that strength leads to more strength.

I am not small and helpless. Remember the little blue engine? Essentially, you have much more power than you think you have. When you feel like a tiny helpless person that self-image is reflected in the nature of your relationships. If you're feeling helpless before an encounter with a romantic love (or a potential romantic love), it's a good idea to take out this card and read it several times. It's particularly helpful if you wrote the card at a time when you were feeling strong and powerful. The memory of

yourself at the time you wrote it can be an enormous
ego-booster.

I am getting stronger and more confident. This card
indicates an on-going process. Any psychological growth
involves a step forward and two back. During the periods
when you feel yourself slipping you need to be reminded
of the overall picture. If you hear yourself saying, "I'm
never going to change," or "I'll never meet the right
man/woman," you need to look at this card.

Better to be alive and hurt, than safe and alone. How
often have you asked yourself, at a particularly difficult
point in a relationship, "Is it worth it?" My answer is,
invariably, yes. As I said earlier, relationships, and the
pain and pleasure they offer, are the essence of enjoying
life. On days when you're not quite sure about the point of
it all, take this card along with you.

My happiness is important. No one is going to place as
high a value on your happiness as you. It's your job to
keep reminding yourself that you have a right to be happy.
You know when you need those reminders. The signals are
very clear. People actually say, "There are more important
things than my happiness." "I'm being too self-involved.
Happiness isn't all that important." Well, there may be
more important things in the world than your happiness,
but those things aren't in competition with your pursuit of
happiness. Children aren't starving, any more or less,
because you want to be happy. You've only got one shot
at this life, and you'd damn well better get the most you
can from it.

I deserve to be loved. If you've been living without an
intense romantic relationship for a long time you may
actually begin to believe that you are somehow "unworthy." People most frequently need the assurance of this
card when they're not in relationships, or when they've
been recently dumped on. If someone leaves you and tells
you, in one way or another, that you don't deserve to be

loved, you must have something to draw upon. Write it on a card. Stand in front of a mirror and say it to yourself. "I am lovable because. . . ." It's especially valuable to be clear and specific about your good, special, unique characteristics. Call up a good friend and ask her to tell you what she likes about you, and why you deserve to be loved. Keep a record of those concrete examples. Those phone calls can be painful and require courage, but we all have the resources to get beyond them.

This card is also valuable when you're in a loving relationship. If you don't really believe that you're lovable, or that you deserve to be loved, but have somehow had the fortune to find your way into a romantic relationship, it's likely that you'll have periods when you suspect that your lover doesn't really love you. During these periods you may feel jealous, or suspect that you're going to be abandoned. You may actually feel like running from the relationship. At times like that you'd do well to read this card before you go home. Feeling unlovable, if you're not careful, can make you unlovable.

Most of the cards I've mentioned so far are designed to help you when you're not in a relationship. But index cards—reminders—are important when you are in an intense romantic relationship. Actually, there may be some overlap, as in the instance of the last card, between the first set of cards and the set I'm about to discuss.

Am I really angry or am I hurt? Before you lay into your partner about something it's a good idea to really examine what's going on. If, for example, your lover forgot your birthday, you may feel furious. But what you're actually feeling is probably hurt. Examine the hurt. What's it about? Do you believe your lover values you less because he forgot your birthday? It's possible, but it's also possible that birthdays (and other such occasions) just aren't very important to him. If they're important to you, you have to let him know that. Remind him when an occasion is coming up. You needn't expect everyone to value the same things you do. The important thing is to avoid the wrong conclusions: He forgot my birthday, therefore he doesn't love me.

Be kind to your love. The whole issue of taking a romantic love for granted will be dealt with in great detail later, but you must always remember how much you value this person, and treat him/her as very precious. I'm not suggesting that you never get angry, or that you screen your dialogue. Rather, I want you to try to keep in mind that the person with whom you're involved is precisely that—a person; complete with fears, vulnerabilities, and longings. It's best to keep this card with you on a day when everything seems to be going wrong—a day when you're likely to take your own frustrations out on whoever is within easy reach.

Express your loving feelings. Perhaps too many greeting cards have over-sentimentalized the idea of telling someone that you love him/her, but the fact is it's a good idea for both you and the person you love. All too often we find it easier to express negative feelings than the positive ones. When we're feeling great and particularly loving we don't say anything, and when things are in less than perfect shape, we talk. The result of that sort of communication is that the emphasis is negative. It's *always* a good idea to express loving feelings when you have them. If you look across the room at your lover and are suddenly struck by how special he/she is, express it. The best time to use this card is if you've been through a particularly negative period. If you've been very critical, or if your lover has been very critical, it's important to remember to express the other side.

Allow myself pleasure. If you really are involved in an intense romantic relationship, chances are you're feeling better than you ever imagined possible. You may, in fact, be walking around with a grin on your face. You may, finally, feel *so* good that you can't tolerate it; in which case you're likely to put a check on those good feelings. As strange as it may sound, many of us get nervous/anxious/suspicious/etc. when we're feeling *too* good. We shouldn't. There's no validity to superstitions that say if you enjoy something too much you're going to lose it. You're allowed to feel good!

Specific Phobia Cards

Beyond the Basic Pack are cards that relate to the disguises I discussed earlier. If you identify with one or more of those disguises, the following cards are likely to be helpful to you.

Checklist lovers. What do I really feel? What do I think I should feel? I can't know what I want until I find it. My old list deprives me of selection. True feelings can't be anticipated. Don't intellectualize.

Let's-keep-it-sexual lovers. Get beyond sex. Share myself emotionally. Sex without emotion deprives me of pleasure. Loving is sexy. Sex and love *can* coexist. I'm scared of caring.

Give-me-some-men-who-are-cruel-hearted-men lovers. I don't deserve to be hurt. I deserve to be happy. I can enjoy tenderness. Let someone stroke me.

Impossible-partner lovers. Available lovers frighten me. Don't get involved with committed people; they only mean trouble. I have a right to a lover of my own. I deserve a full-time lover.

Nice-to-meet-you-let's-get-married lover. Go slow. Take care of myself. Don't squander potential partners; they don't grow on trees. Notice how he/she is reacting to me. He/she can't care for me until he/she knows me.

Super-hostile lover. Hostility depletes me. Express positive feelings more than negative ones. Hold some anger in; loved ones aren't dumping grounds.

I'm-not-good-enough-for-you lover. Do things that make me feel good about myself. My strengths are —————. Stop thinking about my problems and start altering them. I deserve to be with a terrific person.

Ivory-tower lover. The following changes make me feel good: —————. Acting scared makes me feel scared. Everything changes with time, and that's all right. Let my lover help me feel secure.

Time-cage lover. Take a risk. Live dangerously. Let ————— grow. Lack of change is boring. With freedom to grow there's room for deeper love.

Never-care-too-much lover. Give more than I feel comfortable giving. The more I feel, the more I get. Loving brings pleasure, not pain. A limit on how much you give is a limit on how much you get.

Take-me-as-I-am lover. I will feel better if I improve myself. Make it easy for someone to love me. Why don't I want to change for someone? Try to provide in myself what I look for in others.

Work-aholic lover. I deserve to enjoy my life. Relax. I can learn to enjoy pleasure. For whom am I working? I can learn to take care of myself . . . even emotionally.

Beat-your-partner-to-the-punch lover. When I think of leaving it means that I'm afraid. When I think I'm angry, I'm often scared. Hang in there; the impulse to run will lessen. I can survive being left by a lover better than I can survive being a chronic rejector.

Made-To-Order Cards

All of the cards I've discussed so far have had a general appeal. We can all relate to those cards at some point or another. The most powerful cards, however, are the ones that have to do with you, in as specific a way as possible. For example, if you're a "beat-your-partner-to-the-punch lover," you're more likely to be moved by a card that says, "I rejected John and he loved me. Don't blow it with Tom in the same way," than you are by a card that says, "Fight my impulse to end relationships." You, and you alone, know the situations that have pained you, and those situations are powerful when it comes to promoting change.

Virtually every card I've mentioned thus far can be personally tailored in a way that adds to its power. It might be a good exercise for you to select ten cards from either the general pack or the specific phobia pack, and rewrite them so that they apply specifically to you. Use the names of people with whom you've been involved. Refer to specific events that were pivotal in your relationships. Personalizing cards in this way can make old hurts feel fresh again, but experiencing your pain with the intent to change yourself is crucial to forming successful relationships. Your past relationships are your most valuable resource.

In addition to learning to tailor the cards I've given you, you should learn to design cards that address your problems when they arise. The following two case studies give an overview of personality in terms of romantic interactions. Even if you don't identify with the people in these case studies, extend yourself and make believe that you do. The similarities between the following people and yourself are much less important than the ability you develop to focus on problems and take action. As you hone that ability, you'll be able to apply it to your own life.

When you finish reading each case study, answer the questions that follow it and compare your answers to the ones I supply. There are no right or wrong answers in this exercise. The goal is to develop some new insights into how John and Jane, the two individuals discussed below, might have taken better control of their romantic futures.

John

John, a recently divorced businessman, came to see me because he was planning to be married; and somehow, he didn't feel as happy as he thought he should have.

When Elaine, his wife of ten years, walked out on him she said a number of stinging things: she didn't find him sexually attractive; she was fed up with the logical, reasonable way he ordered their life and wanted more passion and spontaneity; she was tired of coming in a poor second in the competition between herself and his work; and, generally, she was depressed to find herself feeling middle-aged when she was only thirty-one years old.

John fell into a despair. He felt totally unattractive. When he looked at himself in the mirror he saw only flaws: he was flabby, he was dull, he was a drone, and on, and on, and on. When he passed a group of attractive women he lowered his eyes and imagined that they were mocking him. After three months of self-inflicted isolation and depression, John got a phone call from Barbara, the receptionist in his office. She said, bluntly, "I've always found you very attractive, and since you and your wife aren't together anymore I thought I might come by tonight and visit."

John's ego had been so bruised by his wife's remarks that he found himself shocked at the idea of *any* woman finding him attractive. And Barbara was a *very* sexy woman. Of course, when he thought about her he knew that she wasn't really someone to be taken too seriously. He felt that she was too different, in background and education from the people in his crowd. She didn't have aspirations of her own and wasn't really all that interesting . . . but her call was titillating and he agreed to see her.

Her visits became frequent and for six months she claimed to have no interest in John beyond their sexual liaisons. The relationship restored John's sexual self-confidence and he began dating other women. Just at the point when John began to feel comfortable with the dating process and with his life as a single man, Barbara announced that she had fallen in love with him and that she wanted more than *just* a sexual relationship. She wanted to move into his apartment.

When John objected strenuously to the idea of living with Barbara she backed down, but continued her campaign on a more subtle level. If she spent the night with him and they had plans to get together the following night, she'd bring a small suitcase. She cleared out a drawer for a few of her things—"Isn't it silly for me to keep bringing the same things from my place to yours, several times a week?" she asked. And John, who was indeed a reasonable, logical man, found himself agreeing. She pressed him to move their relationship out of the bedroom and into his social world and began making dinner parties for his friends.

During this entire period, John's life slipped back into a comfortable, domestic pattern. Barbara made beautiful meals. She added little touches here and there that made his apartment feel homey again, the way it had during his marriage. John began working later because his social life didn't really require the time it had when he was dating and "courting" several women.

Somehow—and he's not quite sure of when—John stopped dating other women entirely. He still didn't feel intensely enough about Barbara so that the choice to be exclusively involved with her could be considered an active decision on his part. Rather, he felt that she was good to him, she validated his sexual attractiveness, and she didn't make great demands on his time. He described himself as being "reasonably" happy, when, in fact, he was slipping into a relationship that would short-change Barbara as much as it would him.

Two months before he came to see me, Barbara told John that she wanted to get married. She said that she loved him, that they had a smooth, easy life together, and that she was thirty years old and wanted to have a child. If he wasn't interested in marriage, she felt that she'd have to end the relationship.

Barbara's ultimatum threw John into emotional turmoil. What was there for him to do? He was afraid to wait for the attainment of emotional fulfillment with a woman. He didn't even trust that there was such a thing in a long-range relationship. He reasoned that he wanted to have a child also, and he certainly wasn't getting any younger. He cared for Barbara and he did find life with her very easy. The idea of beginning the whole "dating" process all over again without any assurance that what he wanted even existed was more than he could bear.

But, and it was a very big "But," he knew that he didn't feel comfortable with this second marriage. He asked himself, "What the hell is wrong with me?" "What do I want?" As John and I talked and he recalled what his wife had said when she left him about wanting more passion and spontaneity, he began to think that perhaps he wanted the same kind of things his first wife had wanted. To be sure, he wanted to be emotionally fulfilled in a marriage relationship. He remembered that she had attacked his "reasonable answers," and said that what was reasonable wasn't always right. "Maybe I want to be—or *need* to be—more irrational," he speculated. "Nonsense," he stopped himself.

Questions on John.

1. A week has passed since Elaine left John and her parting words are still echoing in his head. Write some cards to help him deal with Elaine's voice and the power it carries.

2. Barbara has become a part of John's life but he's enjoying seeing other women as well. Recently he's begun to feel guilty about dating these other women. Write some cards for him to carry when he has a date.

3. Barbara and John are going to have a discussion about Barbara's moving in. John is nervous about losing ground. What are some cards that John might write just before their meeting?

4. Barbara has just given John the marriage ultimatum. His sense of pressure has just quadrupled and the memory of life with Barbara before the ultimatum—the easy pattern

of domesticity—looms large. Write some cards that John might carry with him for the day while he's weighing his options.

Answers for John

1. *Elaine is just one person. Her opinions are just personal opinions.*
   I have a right to be with a woman who values me.
   I'm allowed to be less than all things to all people.
   Because Elaine doesn't find me attractive doesn't mean other women won't.
2. *There's no room for guilt in a really mutual relationship.*
   When I feel guilty, I'm not being straight with myself or Barbara.
   Focusing on Barbara's needs is a good way of avoiding my own.
   I have a right to enjoy other women.
   Because Barbara feels hurt doesn't mean that I'm hurting her.
   I don't owe Barbara things simply because she cares for me.
3. *I know, better than Barbara, whether or not I'm happy.*
   Something is missing in our relationship.
   I can survive Barbara's leaving me.
   I want my private life.
   I am in control of my future.
4. *An easy relationship is not enough.*
   There is such a thing as intense romantic love and I want it.

Jane

Jane was the sort of woman who set out to do things and did them. She was a hard worker and did well in college, went on to a first-rate business school, and landed a job that was the envy of her classmates.

There had been many men in her life, but even the

ones she loved somehow disappeared, or eventually disappointed her. In graduate school she was involved with a fellow student. He was bright but couldn't hold a candle to Jane. Finally, she decided that the competition implicit in their relationship (coupled by the fact that she always came out ahead) was too much of a burden for Stephen to live with. She ended the relationship despite his assurances that he had no trouble accepting her superiority in certain areas of their life.

A year after Jane began her job with an investment banking firm in New York she met Zach at a dinner party. Zach was an artist who had achieved some level of recognition in New York's art scene, and he and Jane were instantly smitten with each other. Their chemistry was stronger than anything she'd ever known. Since Jane had two weeks vacation due her, and Zach could make his own schedule, they decided to go somewhere fabulously romantic together. With less than a week's planning, they flew to Tahiti and had as perfect a time as any two people can have. Jane sent postcards home threatening to never return. She told Zach that nothing else in her life had ever felt as right to her as their time together; and she meant what she said.

When their week was up they boarded the plane to go home. Upon arrival at Kennedy, Zach suggested that they spend the next few days at his loft and Jane laughed. She had a desk piled with things waiting for signature, she had phone calls to make, appointments to arrange, her wardrobe to get in order, a big meeting at 9:30 the next morning. In a word, she had to get home and slip back into what she called "reality."

They made plans for the following weekend, but seized every spare moment for a call . . . just to feel close to each other. Jane found the early-morning calls and hurried declarations of love between business meetings to be very exciting. Their reunion, after a week's separation, was emotional and passionate.

A month after their return from Tahiti Jane got a job offer from the West Coast. It was the proverbial "offer she couldn't refuse." Zach greeted the news with mixed emotions. He was delighted that Jane got such a fine offer, but he was distressed by the notion of her being three thousand miles away. When he expressed his feelings Jane assured him that she loved him and that they'd find a way of working things out.

The next day Zach called Jane at her office. He said he'd been up all night thinking and finally realized that he could move to California also. He loved New York, but he had an agent that could take care of East Coast business and the new terrain might even be stimulating for him, professionally. They could find a place together and have a joint beginning.

As Zach spoke Jane could feel herself become tense. A thought flashed through her mind: could Zach be looking for a free meal ticket? She hated herself for thinking anything quite so ugly, but she'd thought it nonetheless. She told herself that there was nothing she wanted more than to share her life with a man who loved her, but again her thoughts turned sour. Zach would feel needy in a totally new environment and she would be working fourteen hours a day. Maybe *he* was expecting California to be another Tahiti, but she was more realistic; she knew there would be very little time for taking care of a romance.

That night Zach made a spectacular dinner and began talking about their move. Jane finally interrupted, saying that she thought it might be better if she went out to California first, got acclimated to her new job and new environment and *then* sent for him. When he suggested that they might both have an easier adjustment if they were together, she got angry. She accused him of being selfish and of not understanding the pressures of her life. She insisted that if the relationship was worth having it would survive a period of separation.

Jane won her argument, but went home feeling slightly depressed. The next day she officially accepted the new job offer and began preparing for her move.

Questions on Jane

1. Imagine that Jane is back in graduate school preparing to tell Stephen that she wants to break off their relationship. Write some cards that might have helped her if she'd had them in her pocket during that discussion.

2. As Jane was packing to leave Tahiti she felt a familiar twinge: she was distancing herself from Zach. She rationalized that she was preparing herself for the "real world," but on some level she recognized that she was frightened by the intensity of the vacation. Write some cards that she might keep with her on the journey home.

3. Jane knew, even before she told Zach about her job offer, exactly what his response would be. As she anticipated his offer to move with her she began to feel annoyed by him. Write a few cards that might have protected her loving feelings toward Zach.

4. Jane has just returned from her dinner at Zach's. Her own words are still echoing in her mind: "If the relationship is worth saving it will survive the physical distance." She's preparing her briefcase for tomorrow morning and would like to put a card in it to clarify her depression. What might she write?

Answers for Jane

1. *Don't tell Stephen what he feels. He's the expert on his feelings.*
   Work is just one area of life.
   Other areas are as important.
   Look for Stephen's strengths.
   The more rationally I argue the more frightened I feel.
2. *I'm scared that Zach loves me.*
   Risk closeness.
   Don't compartmentalize life.
   I've never felt as good as I do with Zach. Don't lose it.
   Emotional needs are as "real" as professional needs.

3. *Don't push Zach away.*
   My annoyance is a symptom of my fear.
   I'm allowed to have ambivalent feelings.
   Tell Zach that I love him when I feel it.
   Don't lose Tahiti.
4. *The clearer I feel, the more I'm avoiding my feelings.*
   Call Zach before I call my new employer.
   I'm terrified of letting Zach into my life.
   I deserve a full life.
   Don't block sadness. I feel it because I want something.

CHAPTER 8

The Nature of
Vulnerability

UNTIL NOW, all of my discussion of amoro-phobia has focused on the various manifestations of the fear of making oneself vulnerable; but what exactly do I mean by "vulnerable"? Real romantic love is not some vague abstraction. It's a down-to-earth relationship between two very real, flesh-and-blood people who are willing to accept flaws in themselves and in each other. There's something about the nature of this vulnerability that is both liberating . . . and terrifying.

Several years ago some friends of mine described the early nights of their relationship. They'd been friends for a long while before they became lovers, and by the time they finally "consummated" their relationship the sexual tension was at a peak. When they got into bed they were both trembling. Even after they'd made love several times they continued to tremble. "We both knew how right it was," my friend explained, "and we were terrified. It was the scariest, and most wonderful night of my life."

What's So Scary?

What was it about a relationship that felt "right" that terrified my friends? Why do I speak of entering relationships like these as acts of courage? What's the courage about? We've already determined that romantic rejection can't kill you. It hurts; and the hurt can be enormous. It can strike at the very heart of our sexual identity, but most of us do eventually recover from disappointing love affairs.

Fear of vulnerability in romantic love stems rather from the twofold nature of the *responsibility* implied in the relationship: first, a really adult responsibility for yourself; and second, the sense of responsibility that comes with connecting so deeply with another set of feelings.

Let's look at each of those aspects of responsibility more closely.

Responsibility For Yourself

It clearly requires courage to be in the kind of romantic relationship in which you assume emotional responsibility for yourself. This sort of responsibility implies a letting-go of old neurotic behavioral patterns that were less important while you were living on your own (or that may have kept you out of relationships in the past).

Consider the following situation. Marcia and Rick are very much in love. Before her involvement with Rick, Marcia had been in many unsuccessful relationships. Most of the men in her life felt that she was the kind of person who always attempted to blame others— particularly *them*— for other problems in her life. If, for example, she went on a job interview and didn't get an offer, she'd take it out on the man in her life. It was *his* fault because he'd picked a fight with her just before she left for the interview/because he hadn't let her sleep the night before/because he hadn't scrutinized her appearance with enough care/etc.

Shortly after she and Rick fell in love Marcia came up

for a promotion that she didn't get. She was bitterly disappointed and came home from work in a foul mood. Rick was sympathetic to Marcia's disappointment but midway through the evening he was sick of being dumped on. He said, very clearly, "Marcia, I love you and I wish you'd been promoted, but I can't let you take your disappointment out on me this way."

Because Marcia loved Rick, in a truly romantic way, she forced herself to do something she'd never really done before. She made herself *hear* what Rick was saying. Rather than snap back with something about how "little" he understood, Marcia apologized. She *accepted* responsibility for her mood and thereby turned around what had become a very ingrained behavior pattern.

That sort of "turning" is difficult and frightening. Placing the value of your relationship above your fear of assuming *full* responsibility for your own actions is a good "love-meter." With the implicit support of a real romantic-love relationship you can venture into the intimidatingly lonely world of "true listening," and "true growing" and come out the victor. Essentially, it was less hurtful for Marcia to feel the pain of her lost promotion than it was for her to see Rick be hurt by her.

Which brings us to our second variety of responsibility: responsibility for another in romantic love.

Responsibility For Your Lover

Have you ever seen a mother whacking her hysterical baby's bottom and saying, "This hurts me more than it hurts you!"? Well, the baby in this scenario would, no doubt, argue the point, but there's something there.

Loving someone, in a truly romantic way, means opening your life up to twice as much pleasure—and twice as much pain. When your lover is happy, you can experience that happiness *almost* as though it were yours directly. And conversely, when your lover is despondent, the pain you feel can be equally intense.

Is the pleasure worth the pain? As far as I'm concerned

the answer is a resounding "Yes." A truly romantic-love relationship does more than multiply pleasure and pain by two. More to the point, it changes the quality of your experience. The process of "sharing" emotions augments the positive and diminishes the negative. To be sure you experience your lover's pain, but the very fact of your relationship is a source of solace.

Masters and Johnson have defined love as "the exchange of vulnerability." While this is a very limited definition of romantic love, it certainly highlights one of the important consequences of romantic love. The very nature of the relationship implies that you are giving more power over your happiness, sense of well-being and potential misery to one special person in the world than to anyone else.

This exchange of vulnerability is a very important aspect of romantic love. When one's happiness is so dependent upon another person, it's not unlikely that you'd feel frightened. The more intense the love, the more frightening can be the position, especially if there are individual neurotic difficulties complicating matters.

It's always important to tell yourself, and to believe, that there is no better emotional investment you can possibly make for yourself than "exchanging vulnerabilities" with another person in the context of a true love relationship. In terms of potential returns of pleasure, happiness, "wholeness," and a general state of well-being, a love relationship is worth the risks involved.

The Ultimate Vulnerability

The eventual death of a spouse is, unquestionably, one of the things that even the youngest of lovers trembles about at the beginning of a relationship. The unspoken question resounds: Once I let myself need you, how will I ever live without you?

People survive the death of their spouse. I'll discuss this in more depth when I address the issues of aging and romantic love, but to some extent we have to be philosophical. "Is it better to have loved and lost . . . ?" Virtually anyone who has loved will answer affirmatively. People mourn the death of a spouse but they rarely, if ever, wish they'd never been involved.

Surviving partners of the most fulfilling romantic relationships usually find that their relationships continue to sustain their emotional needs even after the death of a spouse. I remember being deeply touched when a client of mine spoke about his grandmother:

"She and my grandfather had a great, great love. They spent all of their time together. They even worked together. I remember, as a child, an almost palpable sense of passion between them. My grandfather died when Gram was in her early sixties and at the funeral she tried to throw herself into the grave with him. No one thought she'd survive without him.

"But in the years that followed I saw her take possession of their life together: as though it were something special she owned that she could take out to brighten up a day. She has hundreds of stories—stories I still love to listen to—and when she tells these stories to us, I get that same electric charge that I remember from being with the two of them. There's nothing morbid or depressing about it. It's just this incredibly rich fiber that runs through the cloth of her life and is still very much a part of it."

Promiscuous Vulnerability

You're probably all familiar with the sort of person who's been hurt in a romantic relationship and uses that hurt to avoid future involvement. It's not uncommon to say, "Never again," while you're still in the process of emerging from a romantic fiasco.

Less common, but common enough to merit attention, are people who consistently move from relationship to relationship and in each instance make themselves roman-

tically vulnerable. These people strike us at once as coura-
geous and, perhaps, a bit careless with their trust. "How
could you have trusted *him*?" we hear ourselves ask.
"You wear your heart on your sleeve . . . no wonder you
get burned," we advise. Finally, we judge privately that
they must somehow, perhaps subconsciously, *like* to get
hurt.

I take issue with that last judgment. I see these "promiscuously vulnerable" people in my practice and with
rare exception, they are *not* masochists. They don't take
pleasure in their pain. They don't want to be rejected.
They want their risk-taking to finally pay off in the form of
a bona fide romantic-love relationship. When they gamble
on a person and their hunch is bad, they rely on great
storehouses of courage and strength to venture back into
the realm of relationships.

Promiscuously vulnerable people are deserving of admi-
ration for their very real courage, but they're in need of
some help. Why do they make so many wrong choices?
What's at the root of their poor judgment?

Most promiscuously vulnerable people want very much—
almost desperately—to be in a relationship. There's nothing neurotic about wanting a romantic-love relationship.
It's healthy to want it. But there's a difference between
desperation and desire.

Desperation

Desperation emphasizes the negative: "I'll never find
someone"; "If I don't find someone I'll kill myself"; etc.
Desire is more positively oriented: "I want to be in a
relationship!" Emphasizing positive feelings actually makes
you a more likely candidate for a love relationship.

The negativism of desperation reflects a low self-esteem
and anger that potential lovers pick up on. These feelings
present themselves almost as a challenge—I dare you to
love me/Are you caring *enough* to love me?—and such
challenges are more off-putting than they are enticing.

Desperation also colors your perception of reality. The

more desperate you feel, the more likely you are to confuse your hopes with your expectations. That confusion can cause serious problems.

Hopes vs. Expectations

Imagine that you meet a man for drinks. You like him and hope he'll call again, but as the days pass it seems clear that he isn't going to. You don't want to call him, but feel disappointed by the lost opportunity for a relationship.

Imagine now that you're feeling desperate when you meet this man for drinks. You come away from the date feeling certain that he'll call you. You *expect* him to call, and each time the phone rings and you don't hear his voice you become a bit more angry.

How might each of the above women react if a month after the drinks the man phoned? Most likely, the first woman would be pleased and open to getting together. The second woman—the desperate woman—is more likely to have built up resentment and express that anger directly, or decide not to see a man who only a short time earlier she had been interested in.

As soon as your hopes become expectations, you become vulnerable. Most frequently people who confuse hopes and expectations suffer the consequences of premature vulnerability. This sort of confusion happens as frequently to people who are in relationships—married people— as it does to single people.

Which Comes First?

Vulnerability should grow from appreciation. Somewhere between "playing hard to get" and "wearing your heart on your sleeve" is a natural process for coming to trust another person. You begin by liking yourself and believing that you have something to offer. As you sense that someone else is touched by the things that make you special, you can let down some defenses.

Unfortunately, promiscuously vulnerable people have a tendency to believe that appreciation grows from vulnerability. It's unrealistic to assume that a stranger will respect/appreciate/love you because you've stripped yourself raw in front of her/him.

The root of the poor judgment that most promiscuously vulnerable people display is a desire to see the world as a good, safe place filled with loving, caring, sensitive people. There's nothing stupid about wanting the world to be this way, and in many respects this world view is preferable to the more cynical view. But at some point you have to come to terms with reality. In this instance reality is the middle ground between two extremes. The world is filled with good and bad people, and you owe it to yourself to be discerning.

Susannah is a woman who understands what her part in a romantic relationship is and is very eager to get things going. Not too long ago she met a man she found very attractive. He was drawn to her as well, and they began dating. Tim and Susannah began spending more and more time together and found that the more time they spent together, the more they *wanted* to spend together. Suddenly Tim withdrew.

One night, after a perfectly splendid evening together, Tim said, "Susannah, I've got to tell you that I love you, but I'm just not the kind of guy that can commit to one woman. I really have this thing about being free and I want you to know about it now because I don't want to hurt you."

Susannah came into session the next day, told me everything Tim had said, and when I questioned her course of action said, "Don't you understand? He loves me. He actually told me he loves me. I'm sure the stuff about freedom will change eventually." She reasoned that if he was feeling anything near what she was feeling he would come to understand, as she did, that their ultimate freedom could only be seen in conjunction with a commitment to each other. From time to time Tim would remind Susannah of his "need for freedom." She'd look at him, ask if he still loved her, and use his positive response as fuel to continue in the relationship.

In fact, Tim meant quite literally what he had said. He cared very much for Susannah, but he wasn't interested in a monogamous relationship. Their relationship came crashing to a halt when Susannah dropped in on Tim one night and found him with another woman.

In the months that followed Susannah talked about how shocked she was that Tim had room in his heart for any sort of involvement beyond theirs. When she talked to Tim the day after her surprise visit he was terribly concerned for her but maintained that he had done nothing behind her back, nothing he hadn't told her he was doing. Still she was shocked. She had hoped that Tim felt exactly as she did, and her hopes became her expectations. Her desires blinded her to reality, even though reality was being presented to her in the voice of Tim.

Susannah mourned her relationship with Tim for some time but met another man, not too long after she and Tim split up and became similarly involved. This man, Jay, was not as up-front as Tim had been. He saw other women but never told Susannah about them. When she began to notice signs of these women in his apartment—a stash of lingerie and makeup—Jay denied that there was anything going on. At one point he offered an excuse by saying that the things belonged to someone he had stopped seeing months earlier, and Susannah—eager to believe the best—accepted the story.

Finally, the evidence became overwhelming and Susannah had to deal with the fact that she'd been duped by a man she trusted and had opened herself up to—for a second time.

One of Susannah's problems was that she hated the cynical tone many of her women friends expressed. She felt so wary of that tone and of the hardness she sensed in these women that she bent over backwards in the other direction. She was shaken by the possibility that her friends were right, that men were all impossible and uncaring and unworthy of trust.

Her desire to fight a cynical world view actually impaired her judgment. That desire, coupled with her desperate need for a relationship, led her from one hurt to another. Once she was able to step back and see a middle ground, she felt much more in control of things.

158   MAKING IT LAST

with such things. Does he no longer find not attractive,

CHAPTER 9

—————

Jealousy and Monogamy

THE VAST MAJORITY of psychologists talk about jealousy as though it were always a neurotic phenomenon. Indeed, jealousy *can* be neuroticized, as in the case of the overpowering, uncontrollable jealousy of a paranoid, but it isn't by definition neurotic. There are times when jealousy is an entirely appropriate emotion. When a threat is imposed on your relationship there *is* such a thing as sane, healthy jealousy. Since all of us, at one point or another, have fallen victim to feelings of jealousy, it's very important to differentiate between the kind of jealousy that's appropriate and the kind that isn't. It's even more important to learn how to deal with the feelings jealousy evokes—the rage, sadness, pain, and crisis of self-esteem—so that they don't consume you.

Appropriate Jealousy

If someone you love very much has stopped loving you and fallen in love with another person, it's likely that you'll feel jealous. You will have suffered an enormous loss, and feel a great, great sadness. It's healthy and natural to not want to lose things you value highly, and there's nothing more valuable than an intense romantic love. Yet you must keep in mind that your mate was under no obligation to love you or to continue in the relationship. As appropriate as it is to feel jealousy, it's entirely inappropriate to feel hostile and vindictive.

When you're in a relationship and are beginning to feel twinges of suspicion and jealousy, the sooner you exorcise them—get them out—the less likely they are to drive you crazy and, in the process, ruin a relationship that might otherwise be in fine shape. Whatever it is that triggers your jealousy must be corroborated by reality, and the best source of reality is, ideally, your lover. It's important, when you talk about jealous feelings with your lover, to differentiate between discussion and accusation. /

Of course, asking someone you love if there's someone else is very frightening. What if the answer is "Yes"? Think about it. If you ask a man you love if he's in love with another woman and if he says, "Yes," what have you actually lost? Your suspicions will have been verified. Your worst fears will have been confirmed. Yet this confirmation didn't precipitate the loss of your relationship. The loss of your relationship, as you valued it, occurred when he stopped loving you and started loving someone else. On an emotional level, he is no less available to you now than he was before you asked the question . . . before you knew for sure that there was another woman. In learning the truth you will have lost the hope that your suspicion might be wrong; but you will have also lost the tension that comes from living with suspicion. You will be faced with a choice of either competing and trying to win back your lover; accepting the situation and waiting for its ultimate resolution; or making the final break yourself.

It's possible, however, that you may feel jealous and ask your lover whether your jealousy is warranted only to hear him reaffirm his love for you and deny the existence of a third party. Obviously there are two possibilities when this happens; the first is that your jealousy is unfounded (we'll discuss paranoid jealousy later), and the second is that your lover is lying. Let's start with the latter.

I once had a client, Andrea, whose husband, Alex, was

a doctor. She never really felt jealous until she received an anonymous phone call from a woman claiming to be Alex's lover. Andrea was terribly upset by the call and became obsessed with the idea of her husband and another woman.

When she told Alex of the incident he totally denied it. He said that she had no reason to feel jealous, that he loved her, and that there was no other woman in his life. Andrea wanted to believe him and did—until she saw him in a compromising position with another woman in his hospital parking lot.

The details are less important than the fact that Andrea's jealousy was compounded by a sense of betrayal. She had been lied to. She felt that she had been made a fool of and for several weeks she felt trapped and paralyzed. Finally, she told Alex what she had seen and he turned ashen. For a long time he was silent, then he began to cry. He told her that he was in love with someone else, but that he still loved Andrea deeply and didn't want to hurt her. He also said that if she could forgive him he would give up the other woman.

Andrea asked Alex if he felt that there was a chance that he might ever be *in love* with her again the way they had been when they first got married. When he said that he wanted that more than anything, she decided to fight, and in this particular case, after a great deal of desire on the part of both Alex and Andrea, they did rekindle feelings they once had. They also came to a new appreciation of each other and developed a kind of trust.

But the outcome is not always positive. Before you can trust another person you must learn to trust yourself. You must have a strong enough sense of self-esteem to emerge from a crisis intact. Healthy jealousy doesn't stem from your own poor self-image. It's focused on the loss of a romantic love . . . a perfectly healthy response to a terribly stressful situation.

Neurotic Jealousy

When hostility, deep fear, and inadequacy accompany jealousy, it becomes neurotic. Your fear of loss overpowers and incapacitates you. You feel unlovable and unworthy of love. Very few people have the kind of authentic, profound confidence in their sexual selves that defies the blow of a rival lover. You may not think you're attractive enough, or smart enough, or successful enough. The specific deficiency is less important than the fact that you view your relationship as a testing ground in which you are always being compared to others. The anxiety that goes along with these feelings leaves little time to relax and enjoy your partner.

A former client of mine complained that whenever he walked down the street with his girlfriend—who was an extraordinarily attractive woman—men would turn their heads to look at her. He said that the attention she attracted drove him crazy and that he couldn't cope with his jealousy. He ended up blaming her for it—"She should dress differently," "She should discourage other men's attention," etc.—and eventually his jealousy and false accusations drove her away.

When I asked him to tell me specifically what made him jealous, he continued to talk about the ogling men. "But she chose to be with you," I persisted. "Another man might have felt flattered that a woman who can obviously attract any man she wants would have chosen him. Why did you interpret the looks of other men as a threat?" My client shrugged his shoulders and pointed out an irony. He said that he only found extraordinarily beautiful women attractive and that he always ended up feeling jealous.

After a great deal of work this man began to probe his reasons for becoming involved exclusively with the kind of women that anyone—man or woman—would turn their heads to look at. These women made him feel important and validated him sexually. He had, in fact, a very low self-image, and felt, on some level, that the world would appreciate him more because of the spectacular ornaments he carried on his arm. He perceived the women in his life in much the way professional military men might view their stripes and badges. They were his possessions. His entire sense of self-worth was terribly precarious because it was derived almost entirely from his association with other people.

This man was always frightened of losing a woman because without her he felt worthless. The fear was so great that he became, essentially, paranoid in his relationships, and eventually his anxiety became a self-fulfilling prophecy. His concern was greater than simply losing a woman he cared for. Along with the loss of a woman, he lost his own identity.

Physical beauty isn't the only thing that sparks jealousy. Someone who's intellectually insecure might view more intelligent people as a source of jealousy. If you tend to feel jealous in your relationships try to focus on what trait the people you're jealous of have in common. Whatever trait you target in on is probably your area of insecurity, and knowing your weakness is the first step in grappling with it. Rather than focus your energies on phantom threats, you can begin to question why you feel ugly, or stupid, or unworthy of being loved.

Neurotic, paranoid jealousy is anathema to intense romantic love. The two sets of emotions are, in essence, contradictory to each other. If you consider the basis of romantic love as we discussed it in Chapter 4, and think about the roots of neurotic jealousy, it's easy to see where the problems of compatability lie. In an intense romantic relationship the commitment is entirely mutual, entirely voluntary, and involves an appreciation of yourself as a totally unique individual. The glue that binds romantic relationships is this mutual appreciation.

The idea of people as possessions is entirely counter to the kind of mutual appreciation I talk about. Possessions exist for the purpose of pleasing their owners. People must be independent in thought and action. If you feel that you want a man or woman to exist exclusively to please you, you're bound to be disappointed. That sort of relationship may work out for a short—very short—time; but we all want to get as much as we give, and we all need to grow and change. There's considerably less assurance of an enduring relationship when you view your lover as a possession than there is if you go the somewhat more frightening path and create a two-individual relationship.

What Do You Do With Jealous Feelings?

Jealousy can be associated with spheres in our life other than love. People can be jealous about work, houses, money, and friends. Yet nothing arouses our most intense and tender feelings in the same way as love-jealousy does. As I said earlier, it's enormously rare to find anyone who has a truly profound sense of self-confidence at the core of their sexual identity. Most of us are terribly vulnerable on the issue of our sexual desirability, and it is just that issue that love-jealousy tampers with. It's no wonder that so many of us, when we are jealous, act in what is obviously a highly disturbed manner.

Whether your jealousy is healthy or neurotic, there are the inevitable questions it arouses. Why did he/she stop loving me? What is it about this other person that's more appealing than I am? What could I have done to prevent this from happening? Is it too late for me to change? Will anyone ever love me again?

The way you deal with those questions is more important than the fact of your jealousy. As I said earlier, most of us have felt jealous at some point in our lives, but not all of us have been consumed by, and diminished by those feelings.

The key to coping with jealousy is twofold. First, you have to accept the fact that someone you love has stopped loving you, and that he has the right to stop loving you. You don't have to be happy about it. You don't have to be gracious about it. But you simply must accept it. Relationships are conditional, and the strongest commitment anyone can offer is a commitment of intent. That point cannot be overemphasized. People's emotions *can* and *do* change over the course of time. The change can make relationships stronger, or lead to their dissolution. That's part of the risk of entering a love relationship.

The second aspect of coping with jealousy relates directly to the questions at the beginning of this chapter. Most of us who are left by lovers feel that we are in some way deficient. Regardless of the face you present to the world, you feel responsible, on a deeper level, for your loss. This assumption of guilt is painful and interferes with potential relationships. There's nothing attractive about someone who feels unattractive.

It is this crisis of self-esteem that's the most dangerous side effect of jealousy. I see it in my practice every day. Not too long ago a woman named Fran came to see me. She had been married for nearly fifteen years when her husband left her to live with a woman he'd been seeing clandestinely for several years. He told Fran that he simply didn't find her attractive, that she was old and set in her ways, and that the new woman in his life knew what it meant to really have fun. They went dancing every weekend, and had a sex life that was so exhilarating that it made him realize how much was lacking from his marriage.

Fran was devastated by the loss. For a long time she refused to go out and meet men. Friends tried to set up introductions, but she begged off. She felt like an old hag. She looked in the mirror and saw only wrinkles and flab. She finally decided to come for help because she was being very actively pursued by a man she worked with who had once been a good friend. Arnie was extremely attractive, three years younger than Fran, and very persistent when it came to getting what he wanted. Fran discussed her anxiety with me:

"He just doesn't stop. Every weekend he asks me to dinner, and every weekend I decline. Last Monday he said that he was going to hound me until I agreed to see him. He says that he's always found me attractive, and it all makes me very uptight. I was thinking maybe I'd take some dancing lessons and then maybe go out with him. I'm all wrong for him. I feel like he's teasing me. He could go out with anyone. There are at least five women in the office who are much better looking and livelier than I am. I just couldn't survive another break-up like the one I had with Joe. And I'm sure that Arnie isn't going to find

me as attractive once he really gets to know me. I like to
have quiet evenings at home . . . reading, watching TV,
or just talking. I don't know what to do.''

I challenged much of what Fran was saying and discovered that she had listened very carefully to what her husband said when he left her. And she made one terribly
disastrous mistake. She believed him. When he said she
was unattractive to him, she became, in her own mind,
universally unattractive. When he said his new girlfriend
was a good dancer, dancing became, for Fran, a prerequisite for having a good relationship.

Essentially, Fran internalized all of her husband's dissat-
isfactions, instead of accepting them as *his* feelings. It's
obvious to anyone who isn't directly involved that because
Joe no longer found Fran to be attractive to him didn't
mean another man might not be obsessed with her looks.
Her crisis of self-esteem was so profound that even when
another man pursued her she found herself unable to trust
him. The idea that there are men out there who prefer a
quiet evening at home reading or just talking never even
occurred to Fran. She was nearly frozen with fear.

We'd all do well to recognize that jealousy in a relationship is an expression of fear, and that sort of fear can
encompass much more than just other potential sexual
partners. People feel jealous of any attention their partner
gives to anyone else. They feel jealous of the time their
partners give to work, hobbies, or anything other than the
relationship.

Such people frequently become ''ivory-tower'' lovers.
They're terrified that any interest, pleasure, or investment
of time in something other than the relationship must
necessarily mean a diminishing of their partner's love. In a
misguided effort to protect their relationships they may
severely restrict their development as an independent individual. In recent years this sort of restricting is commonly
seen among husbands who grow fearful when their wives
leave the home to pursue education or career interests. But
such fear is by no means exclusive to men.

The fall-out of restricting relationships comes in the

form of self-restriction. Many people severely restrict their own interpersonal relationships, their careers, and their choice of leisure activities because they fear that doing what they would in fact most enjoy might damage their relationship. I once knew a woman who had been a champion gymnast while she was in college, but who gave up gymnastics entirely because she didn't think her husband would be comfortable with the idea of her working out on a regular basis with a male coach. She lost something that was an important source of pleasure and pride, and her husband lost the opportunity to live with a woman who had a valuable source of self-esteem. That kind of sacrifice inevitably leads to resentment or boredom; which, in turn leads to problems in the relationship.

Monogamy

I count myself among those who believe that consenting adults have every right to engage in whatever sexual relationships they wish outside of marriage as long as they're being honest. I have no moral qualms with the concept of "open marriage." In fact, I think "open marriage" is probably a very good idea for people who do not have a truly fulfilling relationship within the context of their marriage. It seems very civilized for someone who is—for whatever reason—stuck in a marriage that doesn't serve his/her needs, to have the freedom to openly and honestly seek satisfaction elsewhere.

It is my firm conviction, however, that it's sheer folly for people to engage in extra-marital relationships *if they have the potential for an enduring, fulfilling, romantic relationship*. There's no moral issue involved here. My recommendation of exclusivity is a practical matter, stemming from the enormous value I place on enduring, intense romantic relationships. My professional experience indicates that when you're in an intense romantic relationship, sleeping with other people necessarily jeopardizes that relationship. It's looking for problems.

Just as I wouldn't suggest that anyone play catch with a

ten-carat diamond over a sewer, I wouldn't suggest that anyone in a precious relationship do anything to put that relationship in jeopardy. It's not worth the risk. I'm not suggesting that when you're in a fulfilling relationship you no longer find other people to whom you are sexually attracted. Sexual fulfillment at home doesn't imply a deadening to the outside world! You needn't feel guilty about any feelings—sexual or otherwise—that you have; but you must understand all of the implications of acting on your feelings.

We all owe the truth to our lover. Extra-marital relationships usually involve some degree of deception. We all owe a great deal of emotional energy to our lover. Extramarital relationships must, necessarily, deplete some of that energy. And we all have the capacity to feel jealous, and jealousy, as you've read, can engender all sorts of other complications. There is nothing so devastating as finding out that the person you are in love with has betrayed you or lied to you.

CHAPTER 10

Children and
Romantic Love

PAMELA AND EDWARD had been married for eight years.
Pamela was thirty-two and both she and Edward felt that
the time had come to think seriously about having a family. When they were first married they were absolutely
clear on the issue of having children: they wanted at least
three of them—someday. As "someday" approached, they
learned the true meaning of ambivalence.

It's not that they didn't like kids. The issue was that
they had what they considered to be an extraordinary
relationship. They were as much in love now as they had
been eight years ago. They knew that what they had was
rare, and they placed an appropriate value on it. There was
a nice rhythm to their life that they had become accustomed to, and they were realistic enough to know that the
arrival of a baby would wreak havoc on that rhythm,
replacing it with . . . that was the problem. They didn't
know for sure what a baby would do to their relationship.
It might bring them even closer together, or it might create
tension and make them feel more distant. It was a gamble,
and their relationship was, in their minds, too precious to
gamble with.

The irreversibility of their decision added to its weight. The fact that Pamela was approaching the end of her healthy child-bearing years forced the issue further. That old theoretical "someday" was, in fact, at hand.

The Choice

There was a time when married couples didn't consider the *choice* of whether or not to have children. It was simply what a couple did. It was the given. Fortunately, more and more couples today are approaching the matter of children the way Pamela and Edward did. What's behind all this thought today? For one thing, the cost of rearing children has become overwhelming. Divorce statistics make the home environment seem less stable, and people can't help but think about the burden of single-parenting. Also, young couples can look around and see the way children affect their friends' relationships.

My feeling is that viewing the issue of family as a choice can only mean good things for romantic love. Any decision that affects the *status quo* of an intense, romantic, enduring love relationship requires thoughtfulness and care. You can't decide to have a baby because it will please others—your parents, siblings, clergyman, etc.—without taking into account what you and your spouse want. And when you make a decision, it should be based on mature consideration, rather than fantasy.

I have stressed throughout this book that romantic love is conditional. There's no obligation involved in a romantic-love relationship. The love between parent and child is, on the other hand, unconditional. When you have a child you must love the child regardless of any externals. Children need to grow in a loving environment just as much as they need to be properly fed and clothed. You cannot decide, when your child reaches his second birthday, that he's more trouble than you anticipated and terminate the relationship.

This point may seem very obvious, yet if I were to drop in on Earth from another planet and observe an average family, I'm not so certain that my conclusion would be that most adults recognize their children's need for a loving environment. Unfortunately, having children without being aware of the consequences, both on you as an individual and on your marriage, can lead to a great deal of resentment and loneliness.

If a romantic relationship is to survive children, it's important to ask all the questions that Pam and Ed were asking—and more. It's also important to view the issue of having a family as a question from both the affirmative and the negative points of view. Do we want to have children? Do we want to *not* have children? Either way, you are making a decision. Answering "Yes" to either of those questions means that your romantic relationship will undergo pressure and change.

The pressures a couple undergo when they decide to have a baby are more self-evident than those of a couple choosing to remain childless. The latter couple has to cope with cultural pressures during the years their friends are rearing families, as well as the ambivalence that invariably accompanies such decisions decades after they've been made. Those pressures are no small factor.

No relationship can be frozen in time and preserved. Whether you have children or not, the timbre of your relationship is going to change over the course of your lifetime. The very fact of this inevitable change is what makes the "ivory-tower" lover's plight so futile. To some extent we can all feel empathetic to the fears of an "ivory-tower" lover when we think about expanding a relationship into a family. Of course, the better you know and trust your relationship, the more comfortable you'll feel about its changing. Trusting your lover, and weighing the flexibility with which your relationship has responded to change in the past, relates directly to your ability to emerge from this big decision with an intact relationship. You must be honest with yourself, and honest with each other. The decision has to be mutual if you're going to maintain trust. As soon as you resort to coercion ("Well, if having a child is *so* important to you, I'll go along with it," or

"I'll do all the work and it won't really affect your life too much"), you're in trouble.

The Environment of Love

You know by now that I am not among those who view a romantic relationship as the perfect union of two half-persons into a glorious, glowing whole person. There is nothing, in my view, more important than the matter of maintaining individuality and autonomy in a relationship. If you don't feel "whole" before you become romantically involved with someone, you'll never feel "whole" later.

But there is something almost chemical that goes on between two people when they fall in love. The air around them seems charged. There is a shared rhythm in their movement. Couples in love do seem to some extent to create their own, very private environment. If you have an enduring, intense romantic relationship, the environment you and your lover create becomes your home—regardless of where the two of you may be physically. The environment that springs from your being together is the place in which you can let down all guards, take off your shoes, and relax. It's *that* environment, your spiritual home, that must necessarily change with the addition of a child. You can't help but feel some ripple in the intimacy of a twosome when it becomes a threesome.

This "ripple" is neither good, nor bad. It's simply something that happens. The best thing you can do when you have a baby is anticipate this change and allow for the chemistry of your relationship to change. If you are determined to have things be exactly as they were before, you will inevitably get caught in a futile struggle and, necessarily, be disappointed. If you trust your lover enough to open up to change, if you can relax during the early months and let things happen at a natural pace, you're more likely to be pleased with your new relationship. Fighting the changes that occur naturally when you have a baby is more exhausting than waking up for night feedings.

Breaking In

If you're asking yourself how you could possibly feel a break in intimacy as a result of a baby that was, literally, born *from* your intimacy, you've fallen into a dangerous trap. Most people tend to forget that babies—even infants—are people. They are small people, to be sure, but from the moment they are born they are people: with their own likes, dislikes, needs, and expressions, each of which requires consideration, respect, and energy to deal with.

To some extent, couples with a newborn can expect to feel like they have a full-time, exceptionally demanding, rather ungracious houseguest. If, like most people, you tend to breathe a sigh of relief when someone who's been camping on your sofa for a few weeks picks up and leaves—even if that someone is your closest friend—you can approximate the feeling of very new parents who never get that sigh of relief. The entire situation is compounded by the fact that our culture doesn't really allow any expression of negative feelings on the part of new parents.

A new mother and father are unofficially permitted to complain about their exhaustion. If they happen to have a baby with colic, they can say that they have a "demanding" infant, without inciting the wrath of their family. But under no circumstances does our culture tolerate a new mother saying, "Oh, my God, what did I do to my life?", even when she's feeling that question with every fiber of her being. To make matters worse, she probably feels that she's the only woman who ever felt that way, and her guilt is virtually choking her.

Yet the more you allow yourself *all* of your feelings regarding a baby—including the overwhelming feelings of tenderness—the easier your transition is likely to be. If you and your spouse allow each other to talk about and acknowledge both negative and positive feelings, the issue won't get complicated by layers of guilt. If ever there was a time when open lines of communication were crucial to the survival of an enduring, intense romantic-love relationship, this is it.

I once saw a couple who found themselves in a terrible bind three months after their daughter was born. Each time one of them expressed a negative feeling about the new parenting experience, the other felt a need to defend the baby. When Shane, at eight weeks, began waking to the day at 4:30 A.M., her father became terribly upset. "Why do we have to have a baby that doesn't know day from night? Other babies don't get up this early. I can't stand another day like this with her."

The baby's mother probably felt precisely what her husband was expressing, but came, almost reflexively, to her daughter's defense with something like, "She has a right to establish her own schedule." This sort of response left the father feeling guilty, and the mother feeling like she never got to express her own exhausted annoyance and the difficult schedule she was being forced into. It also created tension between the couple, where they might have had a comradely sense of commiseration.

If the mother had been able to say something like, "I'm exhausted too. This is an impossible schedule, but it's hers," the father might have felt that he wasn't alone with his feelings and at least he and his wife were in a difficult situation together. To some extent, if you work to keep channels of communication with your spouse open, even just after you've had a new baby, you automatically preserve some of the "intimate space" I discussed earlier.

Confusing The Issues

One of the biggest pitfalls an intense, romantic relationship faces with the birth of a child stems from the confusion of "intimate space" I've just discussed. It's not uncommon for either a husband, or a wife (although it's most frequently the husband) to feel excluded while the once-mirror smoothness of his relationship is absorbing the ripples of a newly dropped pebble.

This feeling of exclusion from what has been the most

important relationship in his life is compounded by some hard, physical reality. Reality issue number one is that with rare exception, all new parents are exhausted. No matter how prepared you may think you are for frequent night feedings, diaper changes, formula preparation, burping, and 5 A.M. good-mornings, it is a physically exhausting routine. It's not uncommon for people to push their bedtime up to eight o'clock during the early months of parenthood. If a man feels less exhausted than his wife because they've chosen to divide up parenting responsibilities in such a way that she is bearing the burden, he may have a hard time relating to the exhaustion that brings her day to a close only an hour or two after he gets home from work.

Reality issue number two is that your sexual relationship during the first few months after you have your baby (and in many cases longer) is going to change. Most doctors recommend that women don't have sexual intercourse until after they are examined six weeks after childbirth. For many women, intercourse after the initial period of abstinence is painful and frightening. Men also may feel intimidated about resuming an active sexual relationship, fearing that they'll hurt their wives. For what may be the first time in an intense romantic relationship, sex is likely to take on a tentative, rather than instinctively passionate, quality.

It's entirely possible that the issue of reinitiating your sexual relationship after childbirth may be consistently postponed. Many women simply don't feel very sexy during the time they are integrating their new identity as mothers with their former life-roles. Other women are simply too tired! A woman named Diane came to see me when her son was six months old. She and her husband had had a great love relationship until the baby came, and she felt that they were really floundering. Her husband, Willis, was very resistant to the idea of therapy, so she came alone.

"Willis and I had been together for six years before Adam was born and we were both really clear on wanting to have a baby. We loved each other so much. I never would have believed that having Adam could hurt us. In fact, when he was born, his actual birth was one of the high points of both of our lives. But as soon as we got home from the hospital things started going sour.

"Willis began acting like he was the new baby in the house. He'd get home from work just when Adam was at his fussiest, and expect me to sit down with him, have a glass of wine, and listen to the problems he had at his office all day. I mean, I had this *real* baby that was crying, that needed to be held and fed and patted, and when I told Willis that I couldn't sit down with *him* he'd begin to sulk. He didn't even pay attention to Adam. And if I asked him to do something for the baby, he'd do it in a really begrudging way. Not once in this period did he ever volunteer to take care of Adam.

"The thing that made it all the stranger is that before Adam was born we shared everything around the house. I just wasn't ready for this change. The first time we had sex—which I was really looking forward to—it hurt like hell. I screamed out at one point, and I guess I scared Willis. Because after that he started finding excuses for not having sex. I wanted to talk with him about it but he just said there was nothing to talk about.

"After a while he became more interested in sex, but by that time I was in a rage about how withholding he'd been from me. We tried a few times. It didn't really hurt me anymore, but it wasn't anything too great either. I felt less and less interested; he picked up on that until, after a while, we just lost what had been a terrific sex life. Willis, I think, blames it all on the baby. I blame it on . . . well, what does it matter? We're both busy blaming things on each other, and our relationship is slipping away.

"Now Willis is working late more and more. When I complain about it he says that when he's home I never pay any attention to him anyway so why should I complain. It's so confusing and terrifying. I really loved Willis. Having a baby was supposed to be a wonderful thing we would share, and now I feel like I'm about to become a single parent."

*   *   *

Diane and Willis obviously had unrealistic expectations of parenthood, but their error in judgment was by no means unique to them. It's entirely appropriate for people to anticipate the birth of their baby with positive feelings, just as a couple anticipate their marriage with positive feelings. But positive attitudes must leave room for reality. As problems arise in a marriage relationship they need to be dealt with before a couple resorts to the final solution of divorce. When problems arise from the demands an infant makes on a relationship, they need to be talked about very quickly, before we have the opportunity to store them away and transform them into weapons for later battles.

It's obviously easier to talk about dealing with issues after they arise than it is to actually do it, particularly after the birth of a child when hormones are still ruling emotions, tempered only by exhaustion. Diane and Willis got back in touch with each other by setting up a fairly rigid schedule. They determined as well as they could what their baby's routine was and set aside two hours every night that was specifically for each other. Sort of a standing date. During those two hours they took the phone off the hook and allowed for no interruptions.

One of the things that evolved quite naturally during this period was a series of "think-back" exercises. They talked a great deal about the early years of their relationship and eventually worked their way up to Adam's birth. Eventually, this kind of talking led to the period after the baby's arrival, but rather than feeling like a power struggle, their talking had evolved into a very caring, intimate kind of reminiscence. During the many months that they had these "dates," Adam was blossoming into a full-fledged toddler, and both Diane and Willis found themselves captivated by this emerging personality.

Making Time

I've already discussed the necessity of "making time" for a relationship to endure, but the issue is important enough to deserve emphasis, particularly when we talk about the impact children have on a relationship. Children require a great deal of time, but an enduring relationship requires time also. Diane and Willis found it helpful to set up an artificial structure to insure them time together. As corny as that type of setup may sound to you at first, for many couples it's very often the solution. Time for contact—both emotional and physical—is of primary importance in sustaining a relationship.

Too often relationships get "left-over" time: left-over after work, left-over after friends, left-over after kids, left-over after TV, movies, etc.—and that sort of time is simply not a good enough investment for the most valuable relationship you have. Your relationship requires a prime-time investment, and with the exception of the demands of children who simply cannot care for themselves, no other time investment is as important.

If two people have a sexually satisfying relationship before they have a child, if they are realistic in anticipating the impact of a child on their relationship, and if they allot very regular time for each other during which they talk about what's going on, really listen, and carve out a new intimate environment for themselves, in time the intensely sexual aspect of their romantic love will return—as strong as ever. It's a very natural process that requires a nurturing environment to run its course.

Older Children

It's extremely important to establish the importance of intimacy between yourself and your spouse as early as possible in your child's life. Retaining *your* appreciation of your enduring romantic relationship sets the tone for the way your child will view such relationships, and what kind of relationship you'll have with your child.

There is no such thing as problem-free child-rearing, and, even if there were, it's certainly not the subject of this book. There's no question, however, that a couple who see each other as separate, autonomous, interesting individuals are more likely to allow room for their child's

separateness as well. Conversely, children who grow up
watching the two primary adults in their life treat each
other with respect, are more likely to assume that those
adults should be treated with respect.

None of this means that you may not, at some point,
have a teen-ager who's impossible to deal with. Ideally it
will mean that you'll have children who understand that
there are times when you and your husband or wife will
want to be alone with each other. It may mean that your
children will grow up knowing on some level that sex is
fun, and even more fun in an intense, loving relationship.
The goal here is not to make any moral points. Rather, it's
to allow room in your life—even if you choose to share
your life with children—for the kind of relationship you
want.

PART III

———————◆———————

Making It Last

CHAPTER 11

Surviving Crises

CRISES ARE, essentially, the test of whether or not a relationship is enduring. An enduring romantic relationship is distinguished by the fact that it survives crises. You know by now that such relationships don't offer immunity from crises or a guarantee of "happily ever after." Yet with a great deal of work, patience, and caring, partners who are involved in enduring romantic relationships manage to deal with their crises together and emerge from them with their love intact, or perhaps even a bit more secure than before.

Security Born Of Crises

Many people, by nature, will attempt to rise to a challenge in much the way top athletes love competing against other top athletes. They create the opportunity for tough competition because it brings out the best in them. The surge of confidence and ego gratification that comes from meeting a challenge successfully is thrilling. Even if you attempt to meet a challenge, do your very best, but ultimately don't succeed, you can still feel the exhilaration of your attempt and some gratification in knowing that you tried. At best, a crisis can be looked upon as an opportunity to find your inner strength and put it to use.

Life crises are, in a sense, challenges. Couples that come out of a crisis with their relationship intact have a special bond that grows from their shared experience. Surviving a crisis with someone puts the ordinary strains of everyday life—the power struggle, fears—into a very different perspective. Having survived "the worst," they have a deep confidence in their ability to cope with the ongoing issues of a loving partnership.

There are certain glues on the market for mending broken china that claim to form a bond that's stronger than the original piece. Presumably, if you drop a teapot after it's been repaired by such a glue, it will break everywhere *except* the original crack. A crisis survived by a couple is, ideally, just such a glue.

When I talk about the "ideal" resolution of a crisis and the positive fall-out from crisis-survival, I don't in any way mean to imply that there's anything desirable about having a crisis or that crises are easy/fun/exciting to cope with. I would no sooner suggest that a relationship seek out crises than tell Job to ask God for "just one more test of faith." There are no lives so charmed that they run crisis-free. Trouble finds you without your showing it the way. If you're interested in testing the strength of your relationship just for the sake of testing, I'd sooner probe the reason for your curiosity than "create a crisis." Unfortunately, we have little to say about when our crises come and what form they take. When faced with one, we must apply all of our energies to *identifying it*, identifying *whose crisis* it is, and surviving with the things we value most—primarily our relationship—intact.

Identifying The Crisis

I had been seeing a man who was very much in love with his wife, but who frequently slept with other women. His extra-marital liaisons usually occured when he was out of town on a business trip and he attached so little importance to these sexual encounters that he didn't even mention them in the course of his therapy.

I first learned of them when he came into a regular session trembling. His wife had come across evidence of one such liaison and she was distraught. He was shocked by her strong reaction and terrified at the idea of her leaving him. He described his extra-marital sex as totally meaningless—a habit that dated back from before he knew his wife that he never even thought about—and emphasized that he was deeply in love with his wife.

His wife came to session with him a few days later and gave her view of the crisis:

"I've never loved a man the way I loved Alan. And part of loving someone that strongly meant that I'd never sleep with someone else behind his back. Sneaking around like that . . . it makes me sick to think about it. I trusted him. I never even imagined that he was having affairs. I thought he loved me the way I love him. But he obviously doesn't. If he loved me he wouldn't have been capable of all his screwing around."

Alan interrupted:

"But I do love you. If I had realized that what I was doing would have ended this way, I'd never have done it. None of my screwing around meant a damn thing to me. I was a jerk. O.K.? I just thought it was harmless. It had nothing to do with you or with us. It was a habit from before I knew you that I never bothered to break."

Helen felt that Alan's actions were a clear indication that he no longer loved her. She sized up the situation from the framework of *her own* feelings and arrived, understandably, at her conclusions: If he loved me, he wouldn't sleep with other women. She identified the crisis as a *breach of love*. In fact, that is not what the crisis was about. After a great deal of talking it became clear to me that Alan's love for Helen was not the issue.

Until Helen was able to get beyond her own frame of reference—a framework that defined loving someone as "not wanting to sleep with others"—and accept the fact that Alan was still very much in love with her, they couldn't even begin to deal with the *real* crisis. Yet taking the initial step and appropriately identifying the crisis is enormously difficult. It involves establishing enough distance from your own crisis to be able to view it with some objectivity; and it's hard to establish distance when you've been thrown by a wave of emotional upheaval. But it can be done. When you're gambling with the most important relationship of your life the stakes are simply too high to warrant anything less than your ultimate effort.

Helen agreed to see me because she knew she'd need some outside help in establishing distance. She felt terribly betrayed and vulnerable and believing, once again, that Alan really loved her required more trust than she could summon. She had trusted Alan in the past and had been hurt as a result. But after a great deal of work and enforced hearing—"enforced" by my presence and involvement—Helen began to acknowledge that she did, indeed, still love Alan, and that she wanted to believe again that he loved her. As soon as she was able to let go of her misperception of the crisis, she was able to begin to deal with the real issues.

What was the real crisis? Alan said the crisis evolved from his not appreciating what he had, and not recognizing how fragile his relationship with Helen—like all intense, enduring romantic-love relationships—was. He had to be burned before he recognized the fire with which he was playing. The result of his carelessness was a crisis of trust, which requires a great deal of time and willingness to resolve.

Over the course of a year Helen and Alan began to reestablish the foundation for a new, trusting relationship. Alan had to accept the consequences of having violated their original trust and the tensions that grew from his having been "caught." For a long while Helen was generally very suspicious; and Alan didn't have the luxury of responding to her suspicion with indignation. He had earned it.

*   *   *

There's a childlike fantasy that comes into play when there's a breach of trust. In this fantasy if someone apologizes for a wrong-doing, and that apology is accepted, his misdeed will be eradicated from memory, as though it had never happened. The adult version of that is somewhat different. Loving adults *can* forgive people, and *can* give people the opportunity to act in other ways. But our minds are not chalkboards; they can't be wiped clean with a damp sponge.

Helen could forgive Alan's affairs and could believe that he still loved her. But she couldn't—and should not have been expected to—make believe the breach in trust never occurred. She gave Alan the opportunity to act differently and she continued to love him very much. Alan's sense of how precious his relationship with Helen was became heightened as a result of their crisis. And Helen saw herself respond to a terribly difficult situation with more love and strength than she imagined herself capable of. Their renewed commitment to a relationship that proved to be resilient and comforting would never have been possible if Helen hadn't made the effort to properly identify the crisis as something other than lost love.

Whose Crisis Is It?

A crisis in trust, like the one Alan and Helen experienced, usually stems from the actions of one person, but remains a *relationship-focused crisis*. Frequently, however, a crisis is *individual-focused*. In the case of an individual-focused crisis, the problem belongs primarily to one person, and the relationship suffers the fall-out. It's often hard to keep track of who a crisis belongs to, but confusion over "ownership," coupled by the deleterious effects of crisis fall-out, can be disastrous.

A woman named Janis began therapy because she felt lonely and isolated. She was no longer finding comfort in a relationship that had, for many years, been extraordinarily fulfilling. Janis was a successful lawyer. She and Brad, her husband, a talented academic, were both very career-oriented people who valued their marriage as a loving, supportive haven from the pressures of their professional lives.

Six months before Janis came to see me, Brad, who had been teaching history at the same university for five years, came before his department for tenure review. They were both totally confident that he'd be granted tenure—which meant both approval and security—and they were terribly shaken when he was turned down. Brad, in fact, was crushed by the rejection. It was a stunning blow to his ego.

For six months Janis tried to comfort Brad, but he simply wouldn't allow himself to be comforted. His initial anger quickly turned into depression. He felt as though there were a cloud over him and that his whole life would be a series of failures. If Janis said optimistic things, he accused her of being blind to reality. If she agreed with his view of the gravity of his situation, he accused her of being unsupportive.

Just before Brad went before the tenure board he and Janis—confident about the results of his meeting—decided to try to have a baby. Three weeks after he got the negative news from the board, Janis found out she was pregnant. What began as a major letdown took on crisis proportions. Janis told me about the escalation:

"Brad and I both made a very conscious decision to have a child. We were so excited about it . . . we used to talk about it for hours. But all I could think about when I got the news was that I couldn't tell Brad. I just knew that he'd react terribly—he's getting more and more depressed— and I didn't want him to ruin it for me. I wanted to savor the positive feeling for myself and, I guess, protect myself and the baby from his negativism. And, of course, I was right. When I told him he went nuts. He said that it was the worst possible time, that he was in no shape to be a father, that he was a loser and wouldn't be able to provide anything for a baby, that the baby would just make everything worse. It was horrible.

"Basically, his reaction made it seem as though I had coerced him into getting me pregnant, which wasn't the case at all. I'm thirty-seven years old, though, and I don't intend to have an abortion. What if I couldn't get pregnant again? I'd never forgive myself. And I *want* this baby. Maybe our relationship just isn't what we thought it was. Maybe I'm just not loving enough a person. Everything I do these days is wrong. It's beginning to make me feel like I'll be a lousy mother. I can't even make an adult feel better, what will I do with a tiny, defenseless baby?

"A few nights ago Brad really hit bottom. He said he had no reason to live and that he wanted to kill himself. That was it. I fell apart. I'm beginning to feel *our* baby move inside me and he's talking about killing himself! I felt so incredibly isolated. I don't exactly know how it happened but I started hitting him, really pounding at his chest and screaming, 'No! No! No!' My whole life is falling apart. I hate waking up every morning."

Janis had begun to assume Brad's crisis. Living with a profoundly depressed person is, of course, an enormous strain, but there's a difference between feeling (and coping with) that strain, and taking on someone else's crisis as your own. On the most practical level, Janis had rendered herself impotent. She had always been a strong woman with a very strong self-image, but in adopting Brad's crisis as her own she began to see herself as helpless. With her confidence in her relationship shattered there was really very little reason for her to fight to save it.

It was clear to me that the crisis belonged to Brad. He was having a full-blown crisis of self-esteem, and it was his responsibility to deal with it—not Janis's. When you love someone who's going through a terribly difficult time, your every impulse is to make them feel better. The pain that you see them suffering is painful to you. But the fact is that you *cannot* be responsible for resolving anyone else's internal crises. You can only be responsible for your own. You can care deeply about what your lover is going through, and you can let him know how much you care and feel for him, but you can't kiss it and make it better. As soon as you start believing that you have those magical healing powers, you're in trouble. Simply put, when they don't work, you feel guilty; and before you know it you're in the middle of your own crisis.

Janis and I worked together and once it was established that the crisis was Brad's, she began to feel some of her old strength return. Eventually she confronted Brad with the following: she loved him deeply and felt great compassion for what he was going through; she valued their life together more than anything else; she felt that he was going through a serious crisis that was more than he could cope with alone, and something that he wouldn't allow her to help him with; she couldn't continue living under these circumstances unless she believed that he was making an effort to take care of himself; and that as long as she felt he was, at the very least, trying to resolve his crisis, she would be there for him. She explained that she would interpret his effort to get help as evidence of the value that he placed on their relationship.

Perhaps because Janis was so strong in her presentation of these facts, or perhaps because Brad recognized the truth in what she was saying and was ready to accept it, he agreed to get some help for himself. As soon as Brad began therapy Janis felt like a weight had been lifted from her shoulders. I'm not suggesting that therapy was the only option for Brad, but his willingness to see a therapist symbolized some action on his part to help himself. With the full burden of Brad's crisis lifted from her shoulders, Janis could begin to feel more supportive, and less responsible.

Recognizing that a crisis belongs to your spouse doesn't automatically free you from its consequences. It's not uncommon for your lover's crisis to bring you to the brink of your own. Janis is an example of someone who teetered precariously close to her own crisis of self-esteem because her husband was grappling with precisely that problem. Like so many people who live immersed in crises—their own or their lover's—Janis sought outside help to clarify and resolve her problem. It's very significant, if you are going to understand the nature of crises *and* the nature of relationships, to point out that it was Janis, not Brad, who first sought help. It frequently happens this way.

What Matters Most

In an enduring, intense romantic-love relationship, the relationship—and keeping it intact—*always* comes first. There is really no crisis greater than one that threatens to destroy the relationship; and any crisis that goes unattended will eventually reach such proportions. If Janis had waited for Brad to admit to his problems and seek help before she did, it's very likely that their crisis would have been compounded by a power struggle. This elaborate double-burden is usually more than a relationship—even the most intensely romantic relationship—can bear.

Essentially, when a relationship is struck by crisis the *first* question you must ask yourself is: What do *I* need to do to protect my relationship during this tumultuous time? Alcoholism is an appropriate kind of crisis for illustrating this point. If you're married to an alcoholic you suffer greatly as a result of your lover's sickness. Clearly, the alcoholic needs help; but frequently he or she is the last to acknowledge that there is a problem. In the meantime, if you are to survive to see your lover grapple with alcoholism, you'll need to find a strong support system for yourself: be it a therapist, friends, or a group designed specifically for the families of alcoholics. In order to preserve your relationship (and your sanity), *you* may need help. Ultimately, of course, the burden will fall on the alcoholic; but it's not uncommon for the first move to be made by the "healthy" partner.

Consider a more subtle example. A man and woman have been together for ten years, and during the entire life of their relationship had a very exciting, satisfying sexual relationship. Suddenly, the man becomes impotent. The first time it happens they don't think much about it. After two weeks, however, the tension becomes so great that they both begin to dread the prospect of sex. He feels the fact of his impotence every time he sees her. She looks at him and wants to say, "It's all right. It'll pass," but on some level she really feels terrified. She has no experience with such things. Does he no longer find her attractive? What's wrong with him? Will he get over it? Will she ever be able to initiate sex again without feeling like a castrating woman?

The problem is beginning to spill over into other spheres of their life together. The couple has a son who has problems at school. When she suggests to her husband that he talk to the boy he snaps, "Why me? I can't do anything around here!" He begins to imagine that his wife is looking longingly at other men. The tension is becoming unbearable.

Finally, she cannot cope with the burden alone and, in desperation, she talks to a friend. She cries as she speaks, trembling with the thought that her relationship is falling apart, and feeling guilty for betraying her husband's secret. Her friend listens calmly to the whole story and finally says, "We've been through it too."

The women spend the afternoon talking. The friend's husband had been under a great deal of pressure in his workplace and all the pressure eventually took its toll in their bedroom. The friend goes on to describe how she and her husband, with the help of some good books on the subject, dealt with their problem. They decided to *not* attempt sexual intercourse for three weeks. The conscious decision relieved them of the pressures of "trying" and freed them for intimacy: stroking, holding, kissing. During the moratorium, they found it easier to talk and her husband began discussing his work pressures. By the end of three weeks the tension that accompanied their time in bed together had pretty much dissolved. Not too long after that they resumed their regular sexual activity, feeling even closer and more confident about their relationship for having survived their problem in so loving a way.

When the woman left her friend's house she was feeling a great deal better. Some of her most frightening questions had been answered. She very much loved her husband and felt confident that they'd be able to find their own way of getting beyond their problem—now that she wasn't terrified. The issue for this woman was, clearly, saving her relationship. If she had insisted that her husband "get help,'' she would, probably, have made matters worse. He wasn't the kind of man who felt comfortable talking about his feelings with other men, particularly when the subject was as loaded as "impotency."

Once you know what the crisis is, and who it belongs to, it's time to take action, and the issue of who makes the first move is not nearly so important as the fact that a move is made. If you can recognize some sign of sickness—either in your relationship or in your lover—the earlier you act on it, the better. The longer a crisis goes unattended, the more damage it causes.

Acting On A Crisis

There are three crucial keys to resolving a crisis after you've defined it and determined to whom it really belongs. The first is that you must *keep your lines of communication open*. You and your lover must talk about what's going on. The odds of resolving a crisis with your relationship intact are greatly diminished if you're not open with each other.

Once again, I don't suggest that it's easy to keep communication channels open. It requires a great deal of conscious effort to listen to someone, particularly if you feel betrayed by that person. But if you value your relationship, you will have to simply force yourself to listen. It's as simple—and as difficult—as that.

You may find it necessary to enforce some artificial structure in order to keep communication lines open. It's easy to avoid talking to someone during a crisis. Even if the issue isn't "breach of trust," talking, when you're in pain, is not everyone's first impulse. Many people tend to withdraw when they're hurting. If you and your lover both have an impulse to withdraw, you may need to make a regular date with each other to talk. Early on in this book I discussed the importance of giving your relationship prime-time, rather than left-over time. The issue of time together becomes considerably more important during a crisis.

An extremely successful lawyer I know went through a

crisis of identity around the time of his fortieth birthday. This man had followed a very straight path for his professional life. He went to law school, went to work in a firm, and was eventually made a partner. By the time he was in his mid-thirties, he was earning nearly $100,000 a year and had "arrived." Having "arrived," however, he had some question about whether or not he was really happy. So much energy had been used to get where he was, he never really thought very much about why he wanted to be there. Now, he just wasn't very happy, and his feeling frightened him.

His wife knew that something was wrong, but they never seemed to be able to talk. She was an editor and left for work every morning at 8:30. He rarely got home from work before 11:30, by which time she was exhausted and ready for bed. He often worked weekends, and even when he didn't, there were always distractions. It struck her one day that if they both left the house together a bit earlier than usual, and walked to their offices—which were only a few blocks apart—they'd have a daily block of forty-five minutes with each other, during which the phone wouldn't ring, their kids couldn't interrupt, and they could really talk. It gave him an opportunity to review where he was in life, why he was there, and to think about what he wanted to be doing—with his wife as a sounding board. Which brings us to the second key factor in acting on a crisis.

You must be a willing sounding board for your lover during a crisis; but never allow yourself to be used as a punching bag. There's a big difference between the two. There's nothing particularly evil about wanting to dump your problems on someone else. We all have an impulse to do it at some point or another. If you have a crummy day, you may want to snap at your lover. But you can't act mindlessly on impulse and expect a relationship to endure. However strong your impulse may be to dump the feelings that arise from crisis on your lover, you'll have to stop yourself. Acting out in that way will inevitably bring on another crisis! No one ever resolved a crisis by dumping on his loved one, but lots of relationships have been shattered in the process.

If your lover is dumping on you—under the guise of expressing himself, getting things off his chest, being open/honest—you have both the right and the responsibility to say "ENOUGH!" I once saw a couple that moved from a city to a wealthy suburban community because the husband—Michael—felt a great need to own his own property. Michael was from a very poor family and was driven to be successful. In fact, he made a good living, was doing well in his profession, and had a loving relationship with his wife, Bonnie.

Bonnie came from an upper-middle-class family and was a city-oriented person. She didn't know how to drive a car—and was frightened at the prospect of having to learn—but she felt very sympathetic to Michael's desire to own a home, and over the course of six months she began to get enthusiastic about moving. Michael felt oppressed by the city and was getting more and more mired in a rut; and they both thought the move would lift his spirits and help him underline his accomplishments.

For the first three or four months after the move, Michael and Bonnie were exhilarated. It was fall, and the view from their living room was breathtaking. Michael began preparing a garden for the following spring. When he came home at night he felt like a proverbial king arriving at his castle.

Then came winter, and Michael sensed some old feelings creeping into his consciousness. There were lots of things that needed doing and he never had enough time for them. The driveway needed shoveling; it was dark by the time he and Bonnie got home from work; they never saw their friends who lived in the city; she still hadn't learned to drive, which made her dependent on him. Somehow—and she isn't quite sure when it began—Michael began to seize on the fact that Bonnie couldn't drive as the root of his current dissatisfaction. The same constant state of frustration he felt earlier, when they lived in the city, became Bonnie's fault. He began claiming that if he didn't have to take care of her, he'd have found the time and energy for other things and still be able to relax and enjoy himself.

For a long time Bonnie took his criticism to heart. She felt responsible for his constant uneasiness. She asked him to help her with her driving, but he yelled so much when she was behind the wheel that she found it difficult to function. Finally, with the help of a good friend, she learned to drive and passed her test. After she got her license Michael maintained that her driving was still not safe and insisted on chauffeuring her most of the time.

Gradually, their relationship developed a new tone. Michael complained to Bonnie about nearly everything she did. He began having problems at work, and as those problems escalated, his grievances against Bonnie did likewise. They were isolated in a new community without friends and, ultimately, without each other.

One evening Bonnie was supposed to meet Michael and two friends at a restaurant. Bonnie arrived nearly an hour late, her dress soiled, but very excited. She'd had a flat tire on the highway and, much to her delight, she managed to change the tire by herself. Michael exploded. He began berating her for having the flat and ranting about her incompetence: "Anyone who drives a car should know enough to check her tires for baldness. You probably parked on a pile of broken glass. How stupid can you be? I just don't believe you."

Bonnie excused herself, left the restaurant, and went home. When Michael arrived, on her tail, they had a long overdue confrontation during which she made it very clear that she'd had more than enough. She pointed out that all of the problems he was having now were the same ones that he'd had when they were living in the city; and that they weren't her fault then, and they weren't her fault now. She had tried to listen and be sympathetic, even to the extent of believing that she was to blame, but that she wouldn't listen to another word. She certainly had no intention of being abused by him any longer—either in public or in private.

Even after a half-hearted attempt at therapy, Michael could not accept responsibility for his state of constant dissatisfaction. Finally, they separated, and Bonnie has recently become involved in a relationship with a man who values her specialness. She came to recognize that she couldn't deal with Michael's crisis *for* him; and that unless he dealt with the issues at the root of his unhappiness on his own, they'd never get resolved.

The third key factor in resolving crises should be apparent from all the case studies I've discussed in this chapter. In addition to keeping communication with your lover open, you also need to find an external system of support; be it friends, family, religious counsel, or therapy. There's nothing sacrosanct about any issue that arises from a relationship. Many people tend to feel that by talking about a problem they're experiencing with their lover, they are, by definition, betraying their lover's privacy.

There's a significant difference between idle gossip and trying to resolve a crisis. When the woman I discussed earlier went to talk with a close friend about her husband's impotence, she was talking because she needed help. *Her* need for help and support was as important, and as valid, as the issue of privacy. In that case, *not* talking would have been the equivalent of hiding a problem behind a door and making believe it never really existed. We all have both the need and the right to find effective outlets for our problems. We also have to respect our lover's right to do the same.

Part of feeling comfortable with "outside" support comes from trusting your lover. If you know, on a deep level, that your lover has the relationship's survival in mind, then you needn't be concerned with who he/she talks to. How you seek support is, essentially, your own business. How you attempt to resolve a problem is, likewise, your business. The only thing that matters in a relationship that you both value is that you both try your damndest to resolve crises.

The Crisis and The Relationship—Two Separate Things

Finally, it's terribly important to remember that your relationship is bigger than whatever crisis you may be going through. When you're smack in the middle of a crisis it often encompasses you. You begin to think, "What was our life like before this happened?" Your relationship becomes the crisis. All of your energies are poured into the crisis. All of your time together is spent "dealing" with the crisis. All of your time apart is spent thinking about it.

It's usually hard to bear in mind that a crisis is simply *a specific incident*. It's a powerful incident that can wear you down, but it's not a reflection on your relationship. Even the best of relationships is subject to crises. It also shouldn't consume your relationship. Whether you can talk to your lover about it or not, it probably will be good for you to think back to other times in your relationship and remember all of the positive, special things about your lover that attracted you to him in the first place.

"Think-back exercises," like the ones I discussed earlier, are useful during crises. If you focus on a very happy time, it won't, obviously, erase your crisis; but it will reassure you that there is something special between you and your lover that will still be there for you both when you come out of your crisis. Presumably, you are both the same people—touched by time. These exercises help you to maintain your level of appreciation during a time when it's easy to forget how valuable your relationship really is.

CHAPTER 12

Aging and Romantic Love

THERE'S A POWERFUL CULTURAL BIAS in this country against older people falling in love. Not too long ago a friend of mine began talking about a "problem" he was having with his eighty-year-old father. He prefaced his story by telling me that his father had always been a vigorous, independent, intelligent man—a source of great pride to him—and that this was the first time he'd ever really presented any problem. The "problem" was that his father had a "ladyfriend." My friend explained:

"Actually, *I* call her a *ladyfriend*. My father calls her his *lover*. For God's sake. I'm the first one to believe that older people need companionship, but the man is carrying on with this little gray-haired lady as though he were a teen-ager. Yesterday they announced that they were moving in together and he made some joke about getting a waterbed! The vibes between them are definitely sexual. Really! I find it terribly embarrassing. Now I'm beginning to worry about whether all of this behavior is a symptom of senility."

I found my friend's concern about senility shocking. I said it sounded to me as if his father was in love, and he looked at me as though I were crazy. "Roger," he said, using a tone of voice reserved either for the very, very young or the very, very old, "the man is eighty years old. My mother's been dead for nearly twenty years. He had plenty of time to fall in love when he was younger. At eighty, who's kidding whom?"

We talked for quite a while. I told him about a man in Kinsey's famous study who was well into his eighties and had sex three times a day. Granted, that sort of behavior isn't the norm (enviable as it may be), but certainly there are many examples of public figures who had active sex lives well into their eighties. Why shouldn't his father be entitled to the same pleasures as Pablo Picasso and Bertrand Russell?

Despite a long conversation in which I clearly advocated his father's rights, my friend couldn't swallow the idea of intense, romantic involvements among older people. Even when he reached a point where he could believe that his father was *capable* of a sexual, romantic relationship, he thought that there was something improper about making the relationship public. My friend, who by most standards is a modern man, had a strictly Victorian set of standards that he expected his father to abide by.

Of course, my friend is not alone in his view of older people's romantic lives. If you were to ask a roomful of people in their thirties whether people sixty years and older had active sex lives and intensely romantic relationships, the overwhelming majority would say "no." A few might talk about intensely spiritual relationships and the importance of pleasant companionship; but sex or romantic love would be another matter entirely.

If you pose the same question to a group of healthy people between the ages of sixty and eighty, the response is likely to be entirely different. According to people within that age group, it's not at all uncommon for their relationships to still be sexual. It seems obvious to me which of the two age groups is the best authority on the subject!

I don't mean to suggest that all senior citizens are comfortable with intense romantic love. Unfortunately, the strong cultural bias against romantic relationships for older people has influenced the way many of them view themselves and their sexuality. Many people over the age of sixty feel embarrassed by their romantic desires. They pick up on the judgments of people like my friend and allow those arbitrary standards to interfere with relationships that might otherwise give them great pleasure.

I also don't mean to suggest that senior citizens are necessarily as vigorous sexually as young men and women. But the issue of sexual vigor and frequency is not the same as sexual desire and fulfillment. You may recall my earlier discussion (see page 17) of a client who was a paraplegic but who became involved in an intensely sexual relationship. He experienced sexual pleasure even though he couldn't physically feel it. In much the same way older people who may not have sex in precisely the same way as they did twenty years earlier can still be involved in intensely physical relationships. It may be that my friend's father has a more gratifying sex life than his son—I don't know. But the sexual vibes that my friend picked up on between his father and his father's lover were very much there. Elderly people can be in intensely romantic relationships, and the definition of such a relationship is exactly the same for them as it is for anyone else.

Sickness and Health

Perhaps one reason young people assume that older people don't have active romantic lives is that they confuse aging with infirmity. To be sure, ill health can put a damper on anyone's sex life, regardless of age. But all old people are not sick. Old age is an inevitability; it's not a disease.

Essentially, I apply the same standards for older people that I do for younger people when it comes to romantic relationships. There are senior citizens who are incapable of falling in love; but there are young people who are equally limited. Amoro-phobia can prey upon us all—regardless of our age. Such limitations are much more a product of personality, psychological health, and physical health than they are an issue of age. Why should we expect anyone who couldn't form an intense, romantic relationship in her twenties to discover that capacity in her seventies? If she's spent the last fifty years working out problems, perhaps she may be seeing the light at the end of a tunnel. If she's spent the last fifty years sitting on her problems, it's likely that with each passing year they've become a bit more ingrained.

Many people feel that there just isn't much they can do about their physical health as they age. They look at healthy, vigorous people in their eighties and comment on how "lucky" they are to have retained their strength and energy.

Although we can't control every aspect of our physical health, I believe that there's a great deal we can control. We select our diets; we decide whether or not we will smoke cigarettes; and we make decisions about daily exercise. There's no question in my mind that eating well, exercising regularly, and not smoking, can make a difference in the way you feel as you get older. The fact that you can enjoy intense romantic love even when you're older should be adequate enticement to change your living habits when you're younger!

Aging With A Partner

What about a couple that's been married for forty years? Couples who have been fortunate enough to survive into retirement together face unique circumstances which can be the source of both problems and great pleasure. Consider the situation of Martha and Ira, both in their late sixties.

Ira was an extremely successful businessman, and Martha—as was common in her time—was a full-time wife and homemaker. They both took great pride in their work and in each other. When Ira first started his company they had very little money, and Martha managed to establish a tight budget and stick to it. Her home was always decorated attractively, she prepared sumptuous meals on the little money she had, and she spent a great deal of time with her children. During the early years of their marriage, while Ira was building his business, his work monopolized his life. A few years before he finally retired he sold his now-prosperous company to a large conglomerate for a great deal of money.

When Ira and Martha got married they were very much in love. Throughout the years they remained in love, but they had very little time together. They adjusted to their busy schedules and both believed that they made the most of their time together. When Ira retired, their life changed radically. Martha explained:

"All of a sudden we were together twenty-four hours a day. In the years when Ira was working so much we used to talk about eventually having all this time together as though it would be wonderful. Here we are, together all the time, and we're making each other crazy.

"I think my biggest problem is that Ira is used to being the boss. He was in control of more than a hundred people at his factory. He knew what every worker was doing and how every penny was spent. And I was in control at home. He never asked me questions. It was my domain.

"Yesterday he went to the supermarket with me and it took me three times as long to do my shopping. I keep an inventory in my head; he made me write things down on paper. I have certain brands I buy; he had to read the ingredients on everything. I have a sense, after all these years, of where I get the best value; he had to stop and do calculations.

"Then, when we got home Ira wanted to make love. I was so exhuasted and angry that I called my beauty parlor and made an appointment for a manicure. Anything . . . just to get away from him!

"I know this is a period of adjustment for Ira. Maybe he doesn't feel like he's important anymore. But I never expected it to be such a period of adjustment for me. I thought I'd already been through my retirement adjustment."

* * *

The biggest adjustment couples have to make when they retire involves dealing with vast amounts of time together. People who aren't accustomed to so much shared time have to relearn ways of being with each other. They have to reestablish their togetherness as well as their separateness. Women like Martha, who have been full-time homemakers experience a similar disorientation when their children leave home. They have to find new ways of filling their days that are meaningful. Some women go back to work. Others pursue interests they didn't have time for earlier. By the time their husbands retire they've already made one major adjustment and are probably better equipped to make a second.

Men who retire have to learn to pursue new interests that nourish their sense of self-worth; but, more importantly, they have to learn how to be husbands to wives with whom they spend time. Some men have to get to know their wives all over again. Others just have to learn to cope with another person's pace. Whatever the adjustment is, if it's made within the context of a romantic-love relationship, the ultimate payoff will be enormous pleasure.

Retired couples who make a real effort at keeping communication lines open can use this time of life to renew their appreciation of each other. I've seen many such couples appear to fall in love anew. Men, in particular, who become more involved in their home-life after they've retired are frequently more respectful of their wives.

The same guidelines apply to these couples that apply to young couples establishing their romantic relationship for the first time. The most important factor is establishing a separateness and maintaining individuality. Each person needs to pursue her own interests, as well as shared interests. This psychological separateness make togetherness more interesting and more sexy.

The experiences a couple in love share over the course of forty years are really the essence of a lifetime. Having the time to review your life with someone who's shared it with you can engender enormous tenderness. This tenderness coupled with the excitement of what's yet to come can make retirement an extraordinarily rich time for two people who love each other. Intimacy, extended over a lifetime, can cushion the frightening edge of aging.

CHAPTER 13

Keeping the Spark Alive

I BEGAN THIS BOOK by defining romantic love as the fusion of intense sexual satisfaction and great spiritual affinity; and by asserting that the ecstasy of such a romantic relationship can endure. Romantic love need not be a fleeting rush of emotion. Two people can spend their lives together and continue to desire each other, delight in each other, and find great solace and strength in their relationship. No other aspect of your life can match the all-round potential for gratification of a long-term romantic-love relationship. Nothing even comes near.

But how do you sustain a love relationship? How do you maintain an intense, romantic response beyond the excitement of the first few months?

Settling In

If a romantic relationship is to endure, it's crucial that both partners understand the natural curve of an intense romantic response. Many relationships fall apart because people confuse the settling-in process—the shift from the novelty of beginning a relationship to the familiarity of a more long-term relationship—with a lessening of love.

172

The first step toward keeping the spark of intense romantic love alive is differentiating that spark from the flames. When you first ignite the coals on a barbeque there's a great burst of flame; but it's not until the flames have disappeared leaving a bed of white-hot coals that you can begin to do any cooking!

The flames that mark the beginning of a love relationship are, to a great extent, the result of contrast. The contrast between the way people feel when they're in love and the way they felt before they were in love is extraordinary. One woman told me that a complete stranger standing behind her on a bank line looked at her and said, ''You must be in love.'' She was somewhat started by his statement and said, ''In fact I am. But how can you tell?'' His answer was simply, ''You radiate it.''

Falling in love—finding someone who loves you and desires you more than anyone else—can transform an empty, lonely existence into one that radiates joy. The before and after contrast is extraordinary, and something you are very much aware of for a long time into your relationship. Robert, a thirty-five-year-old man who found himself in his first real romantic relationship, described his awareness of the contrast in his life this way:

''This is going to sound a little crazy, but for the first six months that Laura and I lived together I'd wake up every morning and look at her sleeping next to me and have all I could do to keep myself from crying. I guess I just couldn't believe that she was still there . . . still loving me . . . that she'd always be there. I felt so lucky, and I guess I really felt, for the first time, how empty my life was before. It's not as though I always felt miserable before I met Laura. Actually, it's more like I didn't *know* how unhappy I had been until I had something to compare it with.''

An awareness of the contrast Robert alluded to underlines the intensity of your love. As you settle into a relationship, your measure of contrast naturally decreases. After Robert and Laura had been living with each other for three years, he had more distance from the loneliness he knew before they were together. He loved Laura just as much as he had the day they began to live with each other, but the novelty of their love had given way to a comfortable, easy togetherness. They had come to accept their good fortune as "the way things are."

If you confuse this "settling-in" with a lessening of love, you'll be doomed to a series of short-term relationships that never really reach maturity. Social scientists who claim that the phenomenon of romantic love cannot last more than thirty-six months are victims of precisely that confusion. In Chapter 4, I discussed the difference between "decline of romantic love," and "appreciation decline." If you recognize, and perhaps even anticipate, that the timbre of a relationship changes over the years, and that the "settling-in" process is one such change, you'll be better able to maintain your appreciation of each other and your relationship.

I once had a client who moved to a cabin in the woods with her husband for the first summer after they were married. Her girlfriend, who had been married for nearly ten years and who claimed to be very much in love with her husband, traveled cross-country by herself that summer and stopped by to spend a weekend with my client. Carolyn, my client, was shocked that her friend had made such a big trip without her husband and told me what her friend said when she asked about it:

"Ellie put her arm around me and said that she could understand that I was shocked because Aaron and I were just beginning. She said that ten years ago she would never have intentionally separated herself from Eric for three weeks. But that she desperately wanted to make this trip and Eric just couldn't leave his work to join her. Even though she would have loved to have been with him—and he with her—they both agreed that it was important for her to go. After we talked for a while I began to realize that they really were very much in love, but they were at a point in their relationship that I couldn't yet relate to. The following year we went east and visited Ellie and Eric and

I was struck by the easy, relaxed, loving way they had with each other. It made us feel good about what we have ahead.''

The Real McCoy

I've had many couples come to me over the years and ask me to help them recapture the spark of their romance. Sparks can be recaptured, but only if they were there at the outset. There's no way that two people who weren't intensely in love when they first married can recapture what they never had. If you want an intensely romantic-love relationship to endure, you have to be certain that you're starting out with the real thing.

Part of the real thing you need to start out with in a romantic relationship is a Maximum Sexual Intensity Level—M.S.I.L. It's far more common for people to allow the sexual aspect of their relationship to slide than it is for the spiritual component. I'm not suggesting that sexual desire necessarily lessens; rather, that many people tend to act on their sexual desire less frequently. If you begin your relationship at the peak of sexual intensity, you have a kind of double insurance: first, you can slip back a little bit and still have an intense sexual relationship; and second, you can recall your original sexual intensity with the help of "Think-back Exercises" (see p. 44). It's very sexy to talk about sex with your lover.

Maintaining a romantic-love relationship requires energy. You simply can't be lazy about the things that matter most in your life. Energy, as it applies to the spiritual aspect of your relationship, means keeping lines of communication open. You need to write reminder cards to yourself when you feel those lines closing; but the technique is far less important than the fact that you are vigilant and honest about it.

Energy, as it applies to the physical aspect of your relationship, is even more literal. Without sex there is no romantic love; therefore, sexual activity is something you really can't be lazy about. Anyone who's ever been in a relationship knows the experience of getting into bed and thinking, "Hmmm. I wouldn't mind making love tonight but I'm so tired . . . and I have to be up early . . . and she doesn't seem to be in the mood . . . and . . . and . . . and. . . ." Before you know it the "I wouldn't mind" is covered by a pile of "buts," and you're sinking into a comalike sleep.

The other side of that coin is thinking, "Hmmm. I wouldn't mind making love tonight," and making love. Most of the time, when you decide "To hell with the 'buts,' " and have sex, you end up feeling very glad that you did. You may even think, "We oughta do this more!"

There's an old cliché about sex that says, "If you don't use it, you lose it." And there's some truth to the cliché. The more you have sex, the fresher the feelings are and the more you want it. If you let your sex life slide, your desire can become sublimated—and it's not always easy to get back to where you began.

Time

At various points in this book I've stressed the fact that relationships require a commitment of time. Most of us devote more time to our gardens than we do to the single most important relationship in our lives. If we were to turn the tables and devote as little time to our gardens as we do to our romantic relationships, we'd have mighty slim pickings come harvest time.

A romantic-love relationship both deserves and requires better than left-over time. If a relationship is going to last you have to allocate time for it . . . time to be with the person you love without interruption . . . time to talk . . . time to share feelings and experiences.

For most of us time is at a premium. But what could be more important than keeping the spark of your love alive? Dinner with friends? A re-run of "Lou Grant"? Hemming your son's pants? I recommend that you roll up your kid's cuffs, turn off the TV, and tell your friends that you and your husband just haven't had any time to be alone with each other lately *and want to*. Good friends will understand. It may even start them thinking positively about their own relationship.

The Context Of Long-Term

Earlier in this chapter I referred to a period of transition when a relationship moves on from being "new" into being "long-term." During this transition you lose the novelty and excitement of a new relationship. But you also *gain* a context into which everything that happens will fit. The context is the years of your relationship, the deep knowledge you have of each other, and the experiences you've shared. As this context—the fabric of your relationship—grows, so do your chances of maintaining romantic love.

Consider the case of Mia and Chuck. They had been together for six years before they had a child. For a year after the birth of their son Mia seemed like a changed person. She had always been very easygoing, but now she was almost rigid about schedules. She and Chuck had always enjoyed long leisurely dinners in good restaurants, but now (despite the fact that they had baby-sitters they both trusted) Mia wanted to eat simple meals at home. They had always enjoyed the company of a close circle of friends, but soon after her son was born she became somewhat of a recluse.

Chuck found the changes disturbing and came to talk with me. In our early sessions he expressed a sense of loss. He felt that every aspect of his life had changed with the birth of his son, and he was nostalgic for the way things used to be. But as Chuck talked, he began to develop some insights into what Mia was going through. As his son's first birthday approached, he reported that Mia seemed to be more relaxed and more her old self. He reflected on the year:

"I knew when we decided to have a baby that it would mean lots of changes for us, but I don't think I really

appreciated what it would mean for Mia. A few nights ago
we were talking and she told me that when David was born
she felt like for the first time in her life she was really
totally responsible for another person—and it freaked her
out. She felt like she couldn't be a kid anymore herself . . .
like she had to get her act together . . . like it was now or
never.

"You know, the whole time Mia was going through
these changes I thought a lot about what she was like when
we first met, seven years ago, and how she'd grown
during these years. We've been through a lot together. We
graduated college together, began our first jobs together. I
was with her when her mother died. And I kept thinking,
now I'm with her and watching her become a mother in
her own mind. It was a hard year, but I've got to say that I
feel *so* proud of her."

Long-term love relationships are not defined by what
they are going through in a given moment. In the given
moment of Chuck's relationship with Mia he was very
angry and frightened. He certainly had a right to whatever
feelings he was having, as well as a right to express them;
but if you place an appropriate value on your love relationship, you also have a responsibility to think in terms of the
long-term context of that relationship.

There is such a thing as a neurotic "mood." A "mood"
is not the characteristic state of a person. It's transient.
Usually, it's a temporary negative way of being. It's extremely important for couples to learn how to cope with
such moods, both in themselves and in their partners. As
they grow together and each gets stronger, they'll be better
equipped to tolerate their partner's negative, neurotic
"moods," and may even be able to help their partner
cope. In the context of a long-term love relationship you
develop special sensitivity to each other. You learn when
to allow your lover to be alone, and when to speak up.

The ability to view your love relationship in its long-
term context requires strength and maturity. But then, I've
said from the start that long-term, intensely romantic-love
relationships are for adults. Adults in love relationships

learn to "bring each other up"—all puns intended. They learn to make each other feel good; to make themselves feel good; and to help each other face adult problems like grown-ups . . . with the support of another loving adult.

A FINAL WORD

NOT TOO LONG AGO a couple I know well got married. I saw them a few months after their wedding and they talked about their life together.

"I'm so happy . . . we're so happy . . . sometimes I wonder if this can really be legal. Can anything that isn't forbidden possibly feel this good?"

The answer is, obviously, "yes." The purpose of a love relationship is pleasure. We all have a right to pursue that pleasure. My personal feeling is that we all have an *obligation* to ourselves to pursue that pleasure. We can survive without it, of course, but with it we can thrive.

The first step toward realizing the profound happiness that can be yours in a romantic-love relationship is acknowledging the need we each have to touch, and be touched by another person. In the process we are elevated. It may be, as Shakespeare said, that we are "like flies unto the Gods," but as we extend ourselves to become a partner in an intensely romantic relationship our value, reflected in the eyes of our lover, soars beyond earthly limits.

About the Author

Dr. Roger Callahan was educated at Syracuse University and has studied with Carl Rogers, Nathaniel Branden, and Albert Ellis. He is a member of the American Psychological Association, the American Academy of Psychotherapists, the American Association of Marriage and Family Counselors, and the Society for the Scientific Study of Sex. He has been a psychologist and marriage and family counselor for the past thirty years, and for the past twelve years has conducted workshops on the subject of Romantic Love. Dr. Callahan lives in Beverly Hills, California.

Karen Levine is the co-author of *The Best Way in the World For a Woman to Make Money*. She has also contributed widely to a number of publications including *Cosmopolitan*, *Redbook*, and *Family Circle*.

SIGNET Books of Related Interest